KILLER IN THE HOUSE

Ten Days of Terror in a Pennsylvania Suburb

Kathryn Canavan

Havertown, Pennsylvania

Brookline Books is an imprint of Casemate Publishers

Published in the United States of America and Great Britain in 2026 by
BROOKLINE BOOKS
1950 Lawrence Road, Havertown, PA 19083
and
47 Church Street, Barnsley, S70 2AS, UK

Paperback Edition: ISBN 978-1-955041-66-9
Digital Edition: ISBN 978-1-955041-67-6

A CIP record for this book is available from the British Library

Printed and bound in the United Kingdom by CPI Group (UK) Ltd, Croydon, CR0 4YY

Typeset in India by Lapiz Digital Services, Chennai.

For a complete list of Brookline Books titles, please contact:

CASEMATE PUBLISHERS (US)
Telephone (610) 853-9131
Fax (610) 853-9146
Email: casemate@casematepublishers.com
www.casematepublishers.com

CASEMATE PUBLISHERS (UK)
Telephone (0)1226 734350
Email: casemate@casemateuk.com
www.casemateuk.com

Front cover: The Abt house the morning after the murders. (From *The Philadelphia Inquirer* © 1976 Philadelphia Inquirer, LLC. All rights reserved. Used under license. Photographer Alexander Deans. Photograph provided courtesy of Special Collections Research Center, Temple University Libraries)
Back cover: Abt family photo. (Courtesy of Dr. Bill Haney)

The Publisher's authorised representative in the EU for product safety is Authorised Rep Compliance Ltd., Ground Floor, 71 Lower Baggot Street, Dublin D02 P593, Ireland.
www.arccompliance.com

This book is dedicated to Jack and Peggy Abt and all parents like them who are devoted to their children, work long hours to support them and still find time to love outwardly by volunteering in their communities.

Contents

Author's Note

Imagine two multiple murders happening at the same hour of the same day in two safe suburban towns just four miles apart. Unlikely as that sounds, this is a work of nonfiction. All information and quotations presented in this book come directly from police reports, court transcripts, autopsy reports, IQ tests, school records, prison records, newspaper stories or interviews conducted in 1976, 2022, 2023 or 2024.

The Abt spree murder is one of the Philadelphia region's most notorious 20th-century crimes. A cold-blooded killer broke into a family home, took a seat by the piano and waited for 11 hours. He didn't eat. He didn't drink. He didn't watch television. He slew six innocent people one by one as they came home for the weekend. After each kill, he tidied up for his next unsuspecting victim.

The Vogenberger case, a double murder in a Victorian farmhouse in a time span that mirrored the Abts', was one of the first slayings to involve Taser guns.

A small squad of suburban detectives solved the Abt case in 10 days without benefit of DNA, databases, social media, street cameras, cell tower pings or facial recognition software.

What happened in the Vogenbergers' farmhouse is still a baffling mystery 50 years later. Cold case detectives welcome any information readers might have.

CHAPTER I

Such Unlikely Targets

> Clee and Dechant grew up together in Trevose, and they were always pranking each other. So, when Clee said, "Bobby, I'm over here at the Abt house. I've got two or three dead bodies down here," Dechant laughed. "Stop fucking around," he said. "Bob, I'm not," Clee told him.

My headlights fell on a front yard lit like a movie set. Men bundled in wool jackets and trench coats filled the lawn. Two were bent over inspecting something in the thin snow cover near the front porch. At least one man was working inside a boxy Philadelphia mobile crime van. When I cranked down my driver's-side window, muffled voices flowed in from police radios or walkie-talkies in the distance. I was the only reporter on the scene. My being in the right place at the right time on March 12, 1976, was a fluke.

The only thing I wanted when I pulled into the Trevose 7-Eleven that Friday night was a cold Pepsi. I was headed home from my job as a reporter on a daily newspaper in Bucks County, Pennsylvania. The store manager had become a good source for me because he overheard a lot. He quietly mentioned that two police detectives were in earlier with an odd question.

They wanted to know if any strangers had asked for directions that day.

Luckily, he asked what was up. They told him they were working a multiple homicide at a house less than a mile away. He gave me the cross streets.

Three minutes later, my Toyota Corolla was idling at a steep intersection. The six-pack of squat, recycled-glass Pepsi bottles was carefully seat-belted in on the passenger side.

I had never seen so many police officers at a crime scene in Trevose, a hilly neighborhood in suburban Bensalem Township, Pennsylvania.

I stared at the traditional two-story seated atop a hilly oversized lot. Evergreen shrubs flanked the front porch, and a small fountain dressed up the front lawn, a standard landscape design in the 1970s. Two newish cars and two older models formed a straight line in the driveway.

It was nearly 9 p.m., but the moon was more than half full, so I could see well, even without the floodlights. I watched men's jaws moving, but I couldn't hear any of the words that came out. It was clear from body language alone that none of the busy men on the front lawn would answer a reporter's questions.

I stepped out into the cold anyway because you can't be sure unless you try. Armed with a yellow Bic pen I fished off the floor mat and one of the slim reporter's notebooks stuffed into my glove compartment, I headed toward the crime scene. I got only one foot on the driveway before a man growled that no one was allowed onto the property.

Trevose seemed an unlikely backdrop for a multiple homicide. The woodsy neighborhood had a sweetness to it in the '70s. The narrow streets of mismatched blacktop rose and fell and twisted like a kiddie roller coaster. They were lined with pink mimosa, sumac thickets and weeping cherries spectacular in the spring. Tulip poplars and Appalachian oaks conspired to form an overhead canopy.

Drivers sometimes left the keys in their cars. Children played "Kick the Can" and the tag game "Pom Pom Pull Away." They rode their bikes for miles and headed home when the streetlights came on. The neighborhood was so safe that middle-schoolers regularly pitched tents in a corner yard for outsized sleepovers under the summer stars. No one foresaw that one of the Philadelphia area's most notorious crimes of the 20th century would unfurl there.

What happened at Jack and Peggy Abt's house that Friday was so one-off that it would inspire two episodes of television's *Criminal Minds*.

If I had arrived just 75 minutes earlier, I would have instantly realized the breadth of it.

That was when 21-year-old Michael Abt rolled up the driveway in his new turquoise Ford Galaxie 500, wondering why his mother hadn't answered the phone when he called home to ask her to save him some dinner.

He saw three cars in front of his, but he thought something was amiss because his family's house was completely dark, save the fading fluorescent light above the kitchen sink. By that hour on a Friday night, the whole place usually shimmered with light.

He noticed a missing windowpane just to the right of the lock on the kitchen door. He turned the knob. The second he flipped the light switch, he spotted blood smeared on the linoleum and a blood puddle ahead in the living room. His life began to fork.

His first thought was someone had an accident. It looked like somebody had tried to clean up. Near the piano in the living room, he spotted his little brother Johnny's blood-stained sweatshirt and a pile of blood-soaked towels.

He called out. No one answered. The cold, dead silence struck him right to the bone, he said later.

Never thinking about his own safety, Michael ran through the empty rooms, flipping light switches as he went. He didn't hear a peep. He checked every room except the pitch-black basement.

At nearly 8 p.m., the phone rang. He picked it up. It was ninth-grader Judy King calling for his 12-year-old sister, Kathy. He told her Kathy wasn't home, and he'd have her call back when she got there. Judy thought Michael's voice seemed different than usual, like he was afraid or surprised.

Michael guessed someone had put his hand through the window, and the others had taken him to a hospital. He pulled out the telephone book to call all four hospitals within a short ride from the house. Trevose wouldn't have 911 service for another 15 years.

When his first two calls turned up nothing, he ran across the street to ask a neighbor if she'd heard an ambulance come to his house. Just as Isabel Young was telling a visibly shaken Michael she hadn't seen or heard anything out of the ordinary, a police car came into her peripheral view. It was Patrolman Dave Clee, turning onto Fleetwood Avenue. Clee, a neighbor, was headed home for a supper break seriously delayed because he had brought in four suspects in a roadway squabble. He was three houses away from his dinner when he heard someone whistle.

Seconds later, Michael appeared at his patrol car window. Clearly upset, he told Clee his family's cars were in the driveway, but nobody was home and there was blood all over. Clee went directly to the house with Michael in tow. Mrs. Young followed.

Clee knew the Abts as a nice couple, but, because his own children were much younger than theirs, he didn't know them well. He had never been inside their house. He opened the door to an alarming scene.

The kitchen floor was smeared with dried blood. More blood had trickled down the kitchen walls and crusted on the white baseboards. A large swath of the living room carpet was spongy with blood. Bloody newspapers were strewn about. The steps leading to the second floor were stained burgundy. Michael showed him a blood-sopped sweatshirt. He said it was his little brother's.

Officer Clee led the way upstairs. He asked Michael if it looked like anything had been taken. Michael didn't think so. His stereo was still there.

Clee asked, "Where's your dog?" Michael didn't know. It was as if his family had vanished and taken their 10-year-old Saint Bernard with them.

After checking the rest of the house, Clee passed the two short, saloon-style doors to the basement. He asked Michael if he had looked there. Michael reached for the door. Clee said no. The patrolman pushed one swinging door open a crack and shined his flashlight down. Instead of a sleeping dog, he saw the face-up body of his neighbor, Jack Abt, at the foot of the steps. Blood was coming from his right eye. There was no sign of life. Clee stepped back, startled. He let the door swing back, so the body was out of sight. Michael asked what was wrong. Clee, who knew Michael as a neighbor, told him to just stay away. He said there was a dead person in the basement. Michael asked who he saw. Clee told him he did not know. It was the beginning of a night of terror in Trevose.

Clee realized there were actually three bodies stacked at the bottom of the steps. Two of them had been partially shrouded with a white sheet. He quickly grasped that he had to control a mass murder scene.

Clee's wife, Donna, had spotted his patrol car and wondered why her husband was at the neighbors'. She walked up the Abts' river-rock driveway in the dark. When Clee spotted her near the porch, he gently pushed Michael out the door they had come in.

Stepping away from Michael, Clee quickly and quietly told his wife what he had seen. Donna, a nurse, asked her husband if he had checked the victims to make sure they were dead.

"They're dead, Donna," he said.

Mrs. Young watched in horror as Michael slammed his fists on a car hood, and screamed, "Who is it? My God! My God! Will you tell me who it is?"

Clee asked his wife to walk Michael down the street to their house, roughly a football field away. Soon, a shocked and rambling Michael was joining the Clees' four-year-old and six-year-old at the dinner table. The muscular 21-year-old alternated between hyperventilating and mumbling that he didn't know what had happened to his family.

After a brief time, two officers arrived at the Clees' house to escort Michael to the police station. When he got there, he telephoned his fiancée. He told her that he thought his little brother had been murdered at his house.

Clee had been on the force for three years, but the only bodies he had seen were automobile fatalities, never a shooting victim. Now the 29-year-old patrolman was the first officer on the scene of a gruesome mass murder on his own street, one that would one day appear on the *Philadelphia Inquirer*'s list of notorious slayings of the 20th century. He had to think fast.

He did everything right. He touched nothing, except the bloody shirt Michael had handed him. He managed to keep Michael, who was already distraught, from entering the basement. And, sensitive that Michael might overhear any broadcast on his patrol car radio, he used the Abts' kitchen wall phone to call in the incident. Sergeant Bobby Dechant answered his call. "He thought I was screwing with him," Clee remembered.

Clee and Dechant grew up together in Trevose, and they were always pranking each other. So, when Clee said, "Bobby, I'm over here at the Abt house. I've got two or three dead bodies down here," Dechant laughed. "Stop fucking around," he said.

"Bob, I'm not," Clee told him.

While Dechant was still on the line, Clee realized the stretched-out phone cord was long enough to take another look into the dark basement. He pushed one of the swinging doors open and shined his light down again. He saw more bodies, all with blood coming from their faces. Three were piled at the bottom of the six wooden steps. His eyes followed the blood trails around the basement to others. Stunned, he told Dechant, "Oh, I've got more." Then, "Wait, I've got five dead people. Oh, crap. No, there's six."

Convinced it was no joke, Dechant spread the word.

Ed Keyser, a rookie detective who was in the general area, heard the broadcast and steered toward Fleetwood Avenue. He was second on the scene. Soon, Dechant and other officers pulled up to the house one after another.

Detective Keyser rechecked the upstairs rooms with another officer. He was startled for an instant when he entered one bedroom and came face-to-face with a life-sized wall poster of a popular teen celebrity.

An officer walking the outside perimeter of the house spotted Heidi, the Abts' Saint Bernard, through a basement window. She had collapsed near the exterior basement door, and someone had tossed a jacket over her midsection.

Lieutenant Ted Zajac, who ran the detective division, arrived. When he looked down the stairs, his first thought was, "It's kind of difficult to imagine that somebody would do what they did." It was a freeze-frame no one wanted to keep in the back of his mind.

Zajac called his wife, Pat. "He said, 'A terrible thing happened up here in Trevose. A family was murdered,'" she recalled. "He said, 'There's six bodies here and the dog. I don't know when I'll be home.'"

Lucy Edwards called the police station from her church to find out when her husband, Detective Bill Edwards, would be home for dinner that night. "They said, 'Oh, something has happened. You're not going to see your husband for a very long time,'" she said. "That was the God's honest truth. I didn't."

By 8:39 p.m., Police Chief Larry Michaels had arrived. He could spot at least six victims from the kitchen. Some had rags or jackets over their faces.

No one entered the basement until the medical examiner arrived. There was a reason. "We looked down the cellar, then we kind of backed off," Chief Michaels said. "We really didn't want to screw it up."

Lieutenant Ted Zajac, who ran the investigation, had recently received *Helter Skelter: The True Story of the Manson Murders* as a gift. The book by Vincent Bugliosi and Curt Gentry would become one of the best-selling true crime texts of all time. Bugliosi, who prosecuted Charlie Manson, chronicled the countless missteps the Los Angeles Police Department made at the Manson murder scene. Officers kicked crucial evidence under a chair at the home of murdered actor Sharon Tate. They smudged a fingerprint on the button that opened her front gate. They walked over the killers' footprints. Their blood collection was slapdash. A rookie officer picked up the murder weapon with his bare hands. A TV crew beat police to the bloody clothing the killers discarded in a nearby canyon.

The book had been out for fewer than 27 months when the Abts were murdered, but the LA police's slipups had already become a cautionary tale for homicide detectives across the country. Officers said Zajac was a meticulous investigator though, book or no book.

In unusually savage cases like the Abt murders and the Tate killings, police, even on large metropolitan forces, aren't sure what evidence is important at the outset. They have to reverse engineer it all in their minds.

Officers searched the first and second floors of the Abt house for notes, calendars, phone bills and personal address books that might give clues to the killings. Before email and cell phone contacts, the quickest way to find people who might know a victim was the small, alphabetized leatherette books of addresses and phone numbers that families kept near their telephones.

While they waited for the medical examiner, Zajac assigned detectives to knock on doors for blocks around, hoping a neighbor might have seen someone who didn't belong.

They visited bars and businesses on Brownsville Road, the main commercial artery in Trevose, asking if anyone recalled seeing something one-off.

The Abt family seemed an unlikely target for a spree killer. Chief Michaels would soon tell reporters, "I can see no reason on God's earth why anyone would want to put this family away."

Police had a pretty good idea who the six victims were, even from the top of the stairs:

Peggy Abt, 48, wore her soft blond hair in longish curls. A nephew said she always "dressed to the nines." Peggy was a skilled pianist. She was a well-liked accounting clerk at the Internal Revenue Service's Philadelphia office. A neighboring couple chose her as godmother for their infant son. She coached her daughter's winning baton squad, the Trevose Heights Twirlers. Two of her cousins were Catholic priests, and her younger brother, Bill, was a Philadelphia police detective.

Her husband, Jack, 49, was a tall, stocky man who volunteered as the scoutmaster at the local Methodist church. His brother was a Baptist pastor. Jack installed labyrinthine private branch exchange telephone systems for Bell Telephone. He raised chickens from eggs with his youngest son, and built a coffee table with his middle son. He was the chatty father of five with the easy smile who showed up whenever the local pond froze over, toting a thermos of hot chocolate, building a bonfire, and lacing all the kids' skates. He was no pushover, though.

Just recently, he had lain in wait in the dark to catch two teenage prowlers who had broken his windows and trashed his lawn. He told a coworker he knew the boys' parents wouldn't do anything if he complained, so he'd decided to corner them himself. Once darkness fell, with his huge Saint Bernard standing at his side, he waited silently in the blackness for the teens to show up. Then he coldcocked them.

Lately, he'd been peeved again because someone had tried to smash a small fountain on his front lawn. He enjoyed spreading his folding lawn chair there in the summertime and reading the *Courier Times*, the local afternoon paper, and the *Evening Bulletin* from Philadelphia.

Jack spent his last night in his house reading his newspapers and relaxing in his favorite living room chair. He left the spent papers in the room, where a malevolent gunman put them to use the next day.

Nineteen-year-old Margie Abt worked as a file clerk at FMC Corporation in downtown Philadelphia. Her coworkers there described her as a warm person who was on the quiet side. Her closest friends there knew the pretty clerk with nearly waist-length light-brown hair dreamed of going to nursing school, but she didn't have that kind of money.

Margie had an adventuresome streak. She had flown to Hawaii with one of her brothers' girlfriends the previous year, but it was a disappointing trip because she wanted to explore the island, and the other woman was content sticking around the hotel.

She had already reserved her vacation for the current year. She planned to be off the week of July 12 and the week of August 23.

Garson "Gary" Engle, 20, ate dinner at the Abts' almost every night. He stuck like glue to Margie Abt, his girlfriend of two years. Gary delivered kosher products for Catelli's Meats in nearby Richboro. Despite his long, black wavy hair and his arms tattooed with a skull and crossbones and an ax-wielding hooded executioner, his boss, Tony Catelli, described him as "a beautiful kid." He was nice, mannerly, quiet, and always on time for work. Gary never had a chance to be a slacker. He had been working like a man since he was 12.

At 13, Johnny Abt was a slim but broad-shouldered kid, with hazel eyes and straight brown hair. He was a Boy Scout in the troop his father ran. Johnny taught his school friends how to fish and build campfires and other skills he learned in scouts. His brother Michael was teaching him to shoot the single-barrel shotgun he got for Christmas. He knew how to operate a CB radio, and he was excited that he was about to buy one of his own.

Johnny planned to take the late school bus after classes on March 12, because he was supposed to fight a sixth grader from Cornwells Heights. The kid never showed up, so he rode his regular bus from middle school and arrived home earlier than expected. He walked through the kitchen door shortly after 3:15 p.m.

Twelve-year-old Kathy Abt had twinkling hazel eyes and light-brown hair cut in a long shag. Like the rest of her family, Kathy was tall for her age, almost five feet eight, and pretty and personable enough to attract older boyfriends at 12. She played basketball and ran track. She had a track team meeting that day, so she took the late bus home.

Two Abts escaped the killer completely by chance:

Michael, the tall, blond middle son, missed the killer by a matter of minutes because he came home late for dinner that night. The 21-year-old was an asphalt paver laid off for winter. Like his father, he was outgoing. One neighbor said Michael was the Abt who would never fail to greet him when he passed by the house. Michael planned to serve as best man at a friend's wedding on March 13. He had spent part of Friday afternoon setting up tables at the reception venue. It would be the second time he served as a friend's best man in as many weeks.

Clifford, 23, the Abts' oldest, was at least six feet tall and so lanky and square-shouldered that friends called him "Stein," short for Frankenstein. Clifford sometimes let on it was short for Einstein. He never came home that night because he was serving time at Bucks County Prison.

Clifford's IQ was 111, slightly above average, but his offbeat humor and his cocky manner had landed him in trouble at least since middle school. One of his eleventh-grade teachers took the unusual step of requesting he be removed from her class. Her written request came in the beginning of the 1969 school year, when the television sitcom *Hogan's Heroes* was at the height of its popularity. The show featured American prisoners of war outfoxing a bumbling German commandant named Colonel Klink. "Clifford Abt is a continuous disturbance in my class," the teacher wrote. "He talks continuously and calls people names, including me. Today he called me Colonel Klink."

By the time I came upon the crime scene around 9 p.m., the officers had fanned out to interview neighbors. Peggy Abt's younger brother, Bill Haney, was already hard at work inside a Philadelphia mobile crime van he had driven up onto her steeply sloped lawn. Michael had phoned his Uncle Bill, a Philadelphia detective, from the police station.

Michael also called an uncle on his father's side. His friends did a doubletake when they saw Rev. Lawrence Abt walk into the police station. The stocky, balding pastor of the Calvary Community Baptist Church in Pennsauken, New Jersey, looked enough like his slain brother Jack to be his twin.

I knew none of that when I made the decision to go home without interviewing a single person that night. I didn't know there were six bodies eerily arranged in the basement a scant 60 feet away from my car. They were about the length of a bowling alley away from my front bumper, but I had no inkling of the innocent victims or the odd assortment of 15 items their killer had lined up around them.

I had no clue there were two more bodies just four miles away, either, but no one except the killers would know about them for two more days.

I did know that no matter what I learned that night, I couldn't report anything until Sunday because our paper didn't publish on Saturdays. That meant the Philadelphia papers and the television stations would break the story a full 24 hours before we did, no matter what I did. There were no online newspapers in 1976. No CNN. No YouTube. No Facebook.

I knew I was unlikely to get a scoop that night anyway because I had a history with the police chief. A year earlier, he had threatened to arrest me for aiding and abetting over a different murder story. I didn't back down, because I loved my job and I wanted the story.

I had wanted to be a reporter since I learned to read. My inspiration was a comic strip character called Brenda Starr. We had only one thing in common—red hair. Brenda was a globe-trotting ace reporter who fought communists and the occasional shark or giant squid. I was a kid who played city desk with my dolls, cutting holes in shoeboxes to make desks for them in the ersatz newsroom I set up on the grass under the clotheslines in our backyard.

When my third-grade class went on a field trip to our local newspaper, I knew I was on the right track. The handsome, likeable managing editor ushered my class around the city desk and walked us under the rumbling two-story-high printing press. I was hooked. On the bus back to school, my friends were so taken with the managing editor that they all said they wanted to marry him. I wanted to *be* him.

On March 12, 1976, as I sat in my car in the cold, I reasoned I wasn't going to get a word out of the busy men on the light-flooded lawn. I lived a short distance uphill. The next day was Saturday. I figured I could wake up early on my day off, interview everyone I could find and come up with a good read for Sunday's front page.

I was definitely overly confident when I turned my car around and headed home. I didn't know the number of victims, so I didn't grasp the enormity of what had happened. Seven people walked into the Abt house, but only one walked out.

That seemed unthinkable in a neighborhood so safe that I felt comfortable living alone there in a tiny red cabin in the woods. My rental, fewer than two miles from the Abt home, was built into the side of a cliff above the wide Neshaminy Creek that wended its way around everyone in Trevose. My living room fireplace was carved out of rocks still embedded in the cliff. The avocado-green wall-to-wall carpeting was fitted directly over a rock floor. From the six windows of my galley kitchen, I looked down on the treetops. The rent was cheap because my landlord just wanted someone to keep the heat on so the water pipes didn't burst. There were drawbacks. The cabin was rural enough that a raccoon once made its way into a space above my bathroom and died there, leaving an unpleasant odor and a downward bulge in the cheap ceiling tile for more than a month. My parking space was at the top of the cliff, so I had to hold onto the nylon rope that served as a railing to get up to my car or down to my cabin. My least favorite reporter at the paper warned me that, if I were killed there, they wouldn't find me for weeks.

While I slept, clueless, the news was spreading without me less than two miles away: "There's something going on at the Abt house. They have Action News down there."

Three decades before Snapchat and Nextdoor, homeowners who passed police cars or crime vans in their neighborhood routinely phoned the police station for more information. Bensalem's police dispatchers worked overtime that weekend. They were instructed to say only that there had been a tragedy at the house, and that police were investigating.

Billy Young, who lived cattycorner from the crime scene, came home from a shopping trip Friday night and found his mother crying that the Abts were dead. Billy, a friend of Johnny Abt's, had spent the last two evenings at the Abt house. Days later, the *Camden Courier-Post* wrote all about it under the headline "Billy Was a Lucky Boy." Mrs. Young was quoted saying, "It's just a wonder Billy isn't over there dead with the rest of them."

As the macabre news got around the blocks, some residents refused to open their doors, even to police. Others quizzed detectives at great length before they let them in. "People were absolutely freaked out," Detective Bob Eckert said. He practically had to cram his badge under the door to get one couple to talk to him.

Plainclothes detectives began taking uniformed officers along with them, just so homeowners would open up.

When word leaked out that there were six victims at the Abt house, it raised even more questions for people who knew the family. Neighbors wondered who was slain, because there were seven Abts, not six, and their 19-year-old daughter's powerfully built boyfriend Gary Engle ate dinner there nearly every night. He was usually there by 6:15. Which six of them had been murdered?

At that hour of the night, the police weren't positive either. The only person who knew for certain was the thin man in the leather jacket who walked up the driveway sometime after 8:30 that morning.

CHAPTER 2

The Killer Behind the Wall

People expect things to go bump in the night, but, in 1976, most adults never fretted a killer would invade the sanctity of their home in the middle of the afternoon.

Michael Abt had been the last one to leave the house on Fleetwood Avenue that Friday morning. He didn't notice eyes were on him as he slid into a friend's waiting car. Moments after his ride disappeared downhill, a lean gunman in a leather jacket materialized in the Abts' driveway. The family was about to receive an unwelcome visitor who would change everything.

The man shattered a windowpane in the kitchen door with his gun, reached through the jagged hole and turned the lock. He was in by 8:45 a.m. He cleaned up the telltale glass.

He wavered a few seconds when he heard creaking floorboards upstairs, but then he ventured further into the house. He took a seat by a double window in the light-filled living room to begin what would turn out to be a long vigil. Intermittent faint noises upstairs bugged him. Nevertheless, he waited eagerly for nearly 11 hours. He didn't eat. He didn't drink. He didn't watch television.

When he drafted his plan to kill the Abts one at a time as they arrived home for the weekend, he may not have known how easy his job would be. Temperatures hovering around 30 degrees Fahrenheit made his victims' patterns more predictable. Odds were that family members would head straight through the kitchen to the living room to hang their winter coats in the closet. He would be waiting there for them.

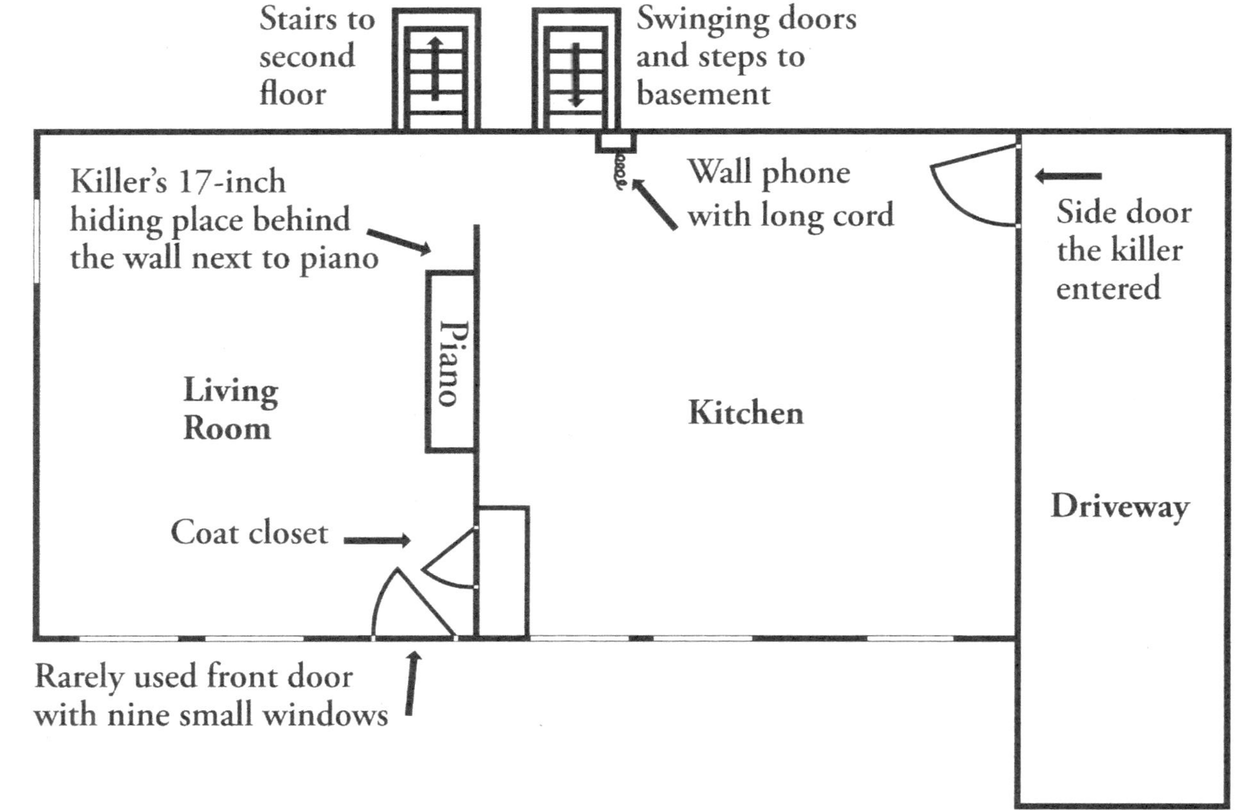

The killer waited in a 17-inch hiding space by the piano in the living room as the victims opened the kitchen door and walked toward the living room where they usually hung up their winter coats.

He had a bird's-eye view of the neighborhood from the windows of the Abts' four-bedroom home. From his perch in the living room, he shouldn't miss anyone approaching either the side door to the kitchen or the front door that the family rarely used.

He was waiting inside a house that Jack Abt had finished with his own hands, installing wallboard and flooring and tile in 1963, just before his youngest was born. She was 12 now, old enough to take the after-school-activities bus home alone that day. Kathy would walk through the side door at about 4:40 p.m., expecting nothing more than her family's customary Friday-night fish fry.

At 10 a.m., the shooter was watching patiently for Michael to come home so he could kill him. Actually, the 21-year-old with longish blond hair parted down the middle was less than a half mile away, but he had no plans to return in short order. He was drinking beer and playing shuffleboard at Sam's Bar, waiting for a friend to give him a lift so he could buy the used Ford Galaxie 500 he had his eye on. The killer would have to wait.

Sometime after 11 a.m., letter carrier William Strange placed the Abts' mail in their post-mounted box near the street. He noticed nothing out of the ordinary.

When Michael pulled up in front of the house in his new Galaxie at noon, the triggerman was ready to kill. He had taken every precaution to protect himself. The grip on his gun was designed to reduce hand fatigue for the repetitive shooter. He donned soft-soled boots to muffle his footfalls. He wore thick dishwashing gloves to mask his fingerprints. He especially feared for his hearing, so he donned a peculiar metal headband with earplugs on either end. To assure he had the upper hand with the four muscular Abt males, he loaded his pistol with lethal hollow-point bullets that mushroom around inside a victim's body.

From his perch inside the house, he could see every move Michael made, but Michael had no way of knowing eyes were watching him from inside his own living room.

The gunman must have felt let down when Michael grabbed his unemployment check from the mailbox and drove off. Now, if the shooter wanted to test his daring plan to kill the Abts one at a time, he would have to wait inside their house at least four more hours until the local middle school let out.

There was an outside chance the intruder would have to deal with an unexpected wild card, too. Although Jack Abt usually worked in Philadelphia, that particular week he was installing a telephone system for a company just two miles from home. He was even closer to home at lunchtime when he and a coworker drove to a PNC bank to cash their paychecks.

The gunman's plan bordered on foolhardy because, at five feet, eight inches tall, he would seem to be at a disadvantage. All the Abt males were nearly six feet tall and square shouldered. Mrs. Abt was five feet nine and a half, an inch and a half taller than the killer. Even 19-year-old Margie, the shortest Abt, was five feet six, and, that day, she was wearing stylish cork-soled shoes that added at least another inch to her height.

The killer was counting on his Strum Ruger to give him the upper hand, though, and he had the element of surprise on his side. He was lank enough to squeeze himself into a 17-inch space between the piano and the living room doorframe. No one would expect a grown man would squat next to a piano topped with children's trophies and leap out pointing a loaded gun.

People expect things to go bump in the night, but, in 1976, most adults never fretted a killer would invade the sanctity of their home in the middle of the afternoon. Certainly not in Trevose, a handful of hilly blocks tucked into a corner of prosperous Bensalem Township. Although it was a scant two miles from Northeast Philadelphia, the open fields and green forests that crisscrossed Trevose signaled that you had entered the westernmost tip of charming and suburban Bucks County.

***

At 3:15 p.m., School Bus No. 50 headed into Trevose with Johnny Abt aboard. Anyone could easily spot Johnny getting off the bus that day, even from a distance, because the seventh grader was just a hair under five feet eleven, and he was wearing rust-colored slacks and a red-and-yellow plaid jacket.

Twelve-year-old Gary Mitchell almost went home with him, but then they decided to meet up the next day and go fishing. One boy did walk Johnny's way.

Johnny's chickens and the white rooster who served as the neighborhood alarm clock made their home in a wire pen at the top of the Abts' driveway. They uncharacteristically flew the coop at least twice that Friday. Both times they scrambled down the driveway and away from the house. When Johnny and the other boy reached the front lawn, they saw the birds roaming close to the street. They chased them back up toward the pen, but neighbors would notice them wandering down the driveway again around 6 p.m.

Once the boys corralled the hens, the other kid walked home, and Johnny walked into a deathtrap.

If Johnny had noticed the missing windowpane in the kitchen door, it wouldn't necessarily have telegraphed danger. He had broken two of them himself. He smashed one to get into the house once. He cracked another unintentionally when a snowball strayed off course. More recently, a neighborhood teen broke one.

Johnny turned the kitchen doorknob sometime before 3:30 p.m. Nothing in the bright and modern kitchen with the U-shaped counter looked askew. But, as he stepped into the living room to hang up his coat, a figure abruptly appeared in front of him. It must have been a puzzling sight. The man was wearing some sort of metal headband. His hands were cloaked in pastel dishwashing gloves, but he held a real pistol in his right one. Before Johnny had a chance to run or fight or even say one word, the shooter fired at extremely close range. The gun was fewer than 18 inches from the boy's face—about the width of a dining room chair. In the wink of an eye, it was over.

The killer intended to drag his 140-pound victim to a far corner of the basement to make room for the others he was expecting, but, suddenly, his plans were violently upended.

All at once, the cat-and-mouse pattern was reversed. In nothing flat, the gunman was the mouse. Seconds after the gun went off, he heard a ruckus on the second floor. It sounded as if someone up there was breaking down a door. He quickly reloaded his gun.

It was Heidi, the Abts' fully grown Saint Bernard watchdog, coming for him. Roused from her rest by the sound of gunfire, she barreled down the six steps to the living room. He fired up at her, but his bullet just nicked the toilet bowl in the bathroom at the top of the stairs. The massive, muscular old dog was gaining on him. He was about to experience a small fraction of the horror he had just visited on Johnny.

The hopping-mad dog chased him around a living room chair. The man fired as fast as he could, bullets spraying every which way as he ran. Five hit Heidi. She chased the intruder until she could take no more of his hollow-point bullets expanding inside her. Then, she tottered into the kitchen and ducked under the short saloon-style doors that led to the basement. Bleeding from her head, she collapsed on the gray concrete floor where she always took refuge during thunderstorms.

Sometime between 3 and 3:30 p.m., Ted Baker drove his blue '67 Chevelle past the Abt house on his way home from high school. He heard no sounds and saw nothing out of the ordinary.

Inside the house, spent bullets, spilled blood and at least one dog tooth littered the living room, but the killer hewed to his plan. He hastily dragged Johnny's long body to the section of the basement underneath the kitchen. He dropped him near the furnace.

Then he crossed over to the spot near the door where Heidi lay. She was still breathing. He fired one more shot. Then he draped a too-small jacket across her hulking carcass to conceal it from anyone who might pass by one of the basement windows.

He rushed upstairs and grabbed one of the bathroom towels to blot the blood that had seeped into the living room carpet. He quickly grasped that there was no way to make the carpet look presentable enough to fool his next victim. His plan hinged on surprise, so he spread Jack Abt's newspaper sections from the previous night over the blood puddles to mask them. The lead headline on that edition was pure coincidence: "Major Crime Up in Bucks: Record Number of Murders."

***

The intruder, his gray pants newly spattered with blood, took a seat near Peggy's piano. He must have shuddered momentarily when someone knocked at the glass-paneled front door fewer than four feet from his seat.

There was no telling who might come to that door, not just because all the Abt offspring from age 12 to 24 still used the house as their home base, but because Peggy and Jack quietly helped others. While they no longer made it to Sunday Mass, they put their faith into action by taking in boys who aged out of a local training school for orphans, and they hosted at least one heroin addict Clifford befriended. They told their kids the temporary houseguests just needed a place to figure out which way is up.

★★★

When Peggy was steering her car down busy 12-lane Roosevelt Boulevard on her way home on March 12, she had no hint an armed man was waiting inside her sunny living room. She also had no hint of another, more pleasant and poignant surprise that she would never get to see.

Shortly after 4 p.m., Dot Lombardo was driving down Fleetwood Avenue when she saw Peggy coming up Dara Faith Drive in her sporty yellow car with the brown vinyl top. Dot slowed her car so Peggy could pull into her driveway. They waved to each other. As a neighbor put it much later, "It was just an average day, except there was a killer behind the wall."

Each car that pulled into the Abts' driveway announced its arrival by crunching the large river rocks beneath its tires. Even if the killer had missed Peggy's Plymouth Duster in his haste, he probably heard it coming, because he did station himself next to the piano again.

Peggy walked up the steps to her kitchen door. Her black faux fur coat covered her business clothes—a black dress accented by a silver bracelet on her right arm, a silver wristwatch on her left, and a double-strand pearl necklace. On her ring finger she wore a white metal band with six crystalline birthstones—one for each of her family members. The greenish-yellow stone was for her eldest son, Clifford, born in August 1952. One of the last things Peggy did the previous evening was to write a letter to him, promising she would visit him at the county prison on Saturday, March 13. She planned to make the half-hour trip with Clifford's fiancée, Shelly Robbins, and maybe Shelly's mother.

When Peggy Haney and Jack Abt went for pre-marriage counseling at Saint Dominic Roman Catholic Church in Philadelphia 25 years earlier, they told the priest they wanted children, and they would happily take all that God sent them. He sent six, but one baby boy, born prematurely, died three hours after birth in 1958. Peggy and Jack flat-out enjoyed their five children, even if Clifford had become unmoored recently.

Peggy's co-workers at the IRS office in Northeast Philadelphia all knew she was anxious about Clifford's problems with the law, although she hadn't told any of them exactly what had landed him in Bucks County Prison that week. They knew Clifford's fiancée Shelly had a child and an ex-husband who was a member of the notorious Warlocks Motorcycle Club. Peggy had told several of them that. They also knew that her husband Jack had celebrated his forty-ninth birthday on March 6, but the milestone was bittersweet because he and Peggy had recently told their kids that he had terminal cancer.

They had kept the bad news close for almost two years, but now his doctor said he had just nine months to live. Jack had told Peggy first—on Mother's Day 1974. They fixed on keeping the family afloat after his death with just Peggy's salary as an accounting clerk. He bought two new cars—the yellow Plymouth Duster and a beige Plymouth Satellite station wagon. He also bought credit life insurance that pays off the debt if the borrower dies. Jack worked carpentry jobs on the weekends to accumulate a bigger nest egg. And, although he recently told a work friend he just didn't feel like his old self, he took a personal day that week to install a new ceiling for his mother. He also spent a recent weekend laying tile in his bathroom.

Despite all that, co-workers Julia Murphy and Bertha Russell remembered Peggy seemed happy on the afternoon of March 12 as she donned her furry coat and walked to her car.

She stepped into her dimly lit kitchen at about 4:15 p.m. The shooter, who had already squeezed himself next to the piano, didn't even wait until she headed for the coat closet. He didn't give her time to spot the bloody disarray in her living room. He leaped out the second she reached the saloon-style basement doors.

He fired four shots into her face in quick succession, blowing his 48-year-old victim backward through the swinging doors. She fell headlong down the basement steps, her IRS employee identification tag still around her neck.

Peggy was still gasping for breath as the gunman lugged her around the basement with so little regard that she suffered repeated blunt impacts to the back of her head. He dropped her face-up near her son Johnny's corpse. Quickly calculating her loud murmurs might tip off his next victim, he jammed a white rag into her mouth and walked upstairs to her kitchen.

She would never get to see an odd tribute from her eldest son. Two days earlier, Clifford had traded a fellow prisoner some cigarettes for some jailhouse art. His new faint-blue prison tattoo boasted a slightly asymmetrical heart, a pencil-thin cross, and the words "Mom" and "Dad."

As Peggy lay dying downstairs, the gunman swabbed her blood from the linoleum floor in her kitchen. Then he took a seat in front of her piano to wait for her children to arrive. Days later, newspapers would describe him as a cold-blooded killer. The term has its roots in the medieval concept that the blood is the seat of all emotion. Passionate people were thought to be hot-blooded. Those devoid of feeling were said to be cold-blooded.

While he was waiting for his next victim, he may have noticed the laminated newspaper clipping that lay on the piano keys. Police later would bag it as evidence: "Abt-Klesh: Mr. and Mrs. Frank Klesh of Goldenridge Drive, Levittown, announce the engagement of their daughter, Candida Jean Klesh, to Michael Abt, son of Mr. and Mrs. Jack Abt of Fleetwood Avenue, Trevose." The announcement featured a headshot of the smiling 20-year-old bride-to-be, a wholesome, model-pretty brunette.

While there was no doubt the killer was cold-blooded, he was plenty concerned for his own safety, so he may have been rattled at 3:40 p.m. when a tapping noise cut through the silence. He had no way of knowing it was Maria D'Ambrosio, the Abts' 13-year-old papergirl, at the kitchen door. She had spotted the Duster in the driveway, and was hoping to collect for delivering the *Courier Times*.

The girl knocked and knocked on the aluminum storm door, but she got no answer. She didn't spot the missing windowpane on the inner door. She did wonder why she didn't see or hear Heidi, the family's Saint Bernard. The dog, whose name the Abts shortened to "Hi," usually barked or at least emitted a low growl whenever a visitor approached the house.

Mr. and Mrs. Abt were always nice. Every time she had collected there she waited in the kitchen while they rummaged around the house looking for some quarters to pay her.

That day, she placed the newspaper in the mailbox and left, figuring she'd return later when more cars were in the driveway. She was eager to finish her collections so she could go roller skating with her friends.

When she stopped at home, Maria told her mother there was a car in the driveway at the Abts' and she knocked repeatedly but nobody came to the door. She said it was weird that the dog didn't even bark. Her mother told her maybe Mrs. Abt was in the bathtub or something and the dog was upstairs.

Peggy's body was actually lying on the cold basement floor by that time. She was gagged, and, at some point that evening, her killer threw an olive-colored jacket over her face and placed her pocketbook by her head.

★★★

If the triggerman scanned the street for his next visitor, he would have noticed a large Sears delivery truck rumble by at about 4:30 p.m. Minutes later, 12-year-old Kathy padded up the driveway for the last time. She was wearing blue jeans and a white T-shirt with writing on it under a navy-blue hip-length coat with a gold buckle in the front. Her only jewelry was a gold necklace. She was wearing brown Earth Shoes, a popular '70s style that featured heels lower than the soles, so you felt as if you were walking in the sand.

Kathy was a seventh grader at Neil Armstrong Middle School, just like her brother Johnny. Some people thought they were twins. Her best subject was physical education, where she earned an "A." A girl in her gym class told police that Kathy was nice to everyone, not mean like some of the popular girls.

If she didn't have a track team meeting that Friday, she would have taken the same bus as her brother, and they would have entered the house together. As it happened, she left school at 4:20 p.m. on Bus No. 43. She took a seat directly across from Karen Thorpe for the 15-minute ride to Trevose. As the bus neared Kathy's stop at 4:35 p.m., Karen said, "See you Monday." Kathy said it back, "See you Monday."

Kathy entered the house through the kitchen door and passed by the swinging doors to the basement, blithely unaware a man was counting her steps. Then everything veered.

Just as the child was about to enter the living room, her executioner pounced. Her mouth was open, but she had no time to scream. He fired twice into her small face, holding the gun even closer than he had with her mother and brother, so close that cinder-like particles of unburned gunpowder dotted the inside of her throat. She fell to the floor still alive. He carried her to the basement and dropped her next to her mother. She gasped and moaned, so he stuffed a rag into her mouth to shut her up. Then he fired a third bullet into her head.

He hurried back to the kitchen where he repeated all his usual steps to hide the slaughter.

★★★

If the gunman had surveilled his victims in the days immediately prior to the slayings, he knew Jack was working minutes away from home that week and he usually pulled up the driveway between 4:45 and 5 p.m. He had to be in his spot by the piano by then.

Things broke the gunman's way. Jack was a few minutes behind schedule that night. He steered his station wagon out of the employee parking lot at about 4:48 p.m. He would likely be home around 5:04, unless he stopped to buy beer for the weekend.

Jack was looking forward to finishing some projects around the house that weekend. He didn't let his cancer stop him from making repairs while he still could. He still volunteered as a scoutmaster, too.

Around the same week he had to tell his kids about his cancer, one of the scouts in his troop was picked up by the police. Scared to call his own father, the boy used his phone call to reach Jack, who drove him home and helped him explain to his parents.

Even as teens, Jack's sons' friends still thought he was a cool dad. When they learned to drive, he showed them how to backfire their cars to make loud popping noises just for fun.

A family story had Jack driving his old high-performance Buick Special Sport Wagon through New Jersey's massive Pine Barrens to his favorite surf fishing spot on Long Beach Island, a fish-rich barrier island off the Jersey shore. A state trooper stops him and says the road is closed because a section of the million-acre pine forest is afire. It was Jack's day off, and he wanted to catch some bluefish and striped bass. He took full advantage of his V-8 Wildcat engine and blew past the officer. He got his fish.

Jack kept a .22 revolver in his house, and neighbors said the World War II vet was the kind of man who absolutely would fight if confronted by a gunman.

Jack had two separate $15,000 life insurance policies. One was a double indemnity policy, but it wouldn't pay double for cancer, only for an accidental death or homicide.

The gunman might have preemptively squatted aside the piano if he heard a car wheeling past the house at 5 p.m. that Friday, but it wasn't Jack. It was Ed Cooney, who lived down the street. He was going bowling.

Jack's station wagon pulled onto Fleetwood Avenue a few minutes after that. The killer eyed it as it turned into the driveway, but events briefly shifted out of his control. He could hear Jack talking with someone, but he couldn't see who it was, and he couldn't make out any words. He couldn't be sure whether one large man would be coming his way, or perhaps two.

The gunman could relax. The other voice in the driveway belonged to Maria D'Ambrosio, the papergirl who was still working her route.

She had spotted Jack's station wagon, and she asked if he would mind if she collected off him.

For the first time since she began delivering there, she happened to catch Jack in his driveway and he happened to have enough change in the front pocket of his coat to pay her, so she didn't need to enter the house. She took the coins and left. He headed into his house. She didn't notice anything out of the ordinary.

Because Jack never had to enter the house to get cash to pay her, everything lined up for the gunman. It also lined up for Maria. She was halfway down the driveway by the time Jack turned the kitchen doorknob. She was too far away to hear anything, blissfully unaware of her close brush with death.

Jack walked into a too-quiet kitchen. Seeing Peggy's Duster in the driveway, he must have wondered where she was. He had spent part of his lunch hour at Two Guys Discount Department Store looking for a record she liked. He was a breath or two away from death as he approached the swinging basement doors.

He was headed for the coat closet in the living room, but he never made it past the spot where his wife had been ambushed an hour earlier. Without any warning, the killer burst from behind the living room wall pointing a pistol. There may have been a whoosh of recognition before the shooter with the light-brown hair fired into Jack's right eye at extremely close range.

The thin man shoved the homeowner down the basement steps, still wearing his office attire and his tan winter coat with the furry lining. His wallet was still lodged in the right rear pocket of his dark blue pants. With Jack out of the picture, the triggerman had about an hour to kill before his next victim walked up the driveway, but, of course, he had no way of knowing that.

***

It was 5:15 p.m., and four of the Abts were dead. If the gunman knew the family's Friday-night routine, he might have been expecting both

Margie and Michael at any moment. The light-colored wall phone in the kitchen rang six times at 5:45 p.m., adding to the frenzy.

The killer needn't have fretted. That particular Friday night, Michael was still setting up for his friend's wedding, and he still needed to pick something up at another friend's house in nearby Oakford.

Margie would come through the kitchen door next because she had rushed from her center-city office building to Suburban Station to catch the 5:13 p.m. commuter train to Trevose Station.

She had a celebratory day on March 12. Friday was her office payday, so she and her friend Caren Foster cashed their checks at Fidelity Bank and lunched at an Italian restaurant. At lunch, Margie mentioned Gary was taking her to Rustler for dinner that night to celebrate their second anniversary as a couple.

It would be Margie's second trip to the Western-themed budget steakhouse in two days. She went there the previous night with her best friend since kindergarten. When the teenagers returned to the Abts' afterward, Peggy yelled down to them from upstairs, teasing them about going to Rustler. She joked that they should have gone to a more expensive place and found a couple of nice guys to pick up the tab.

At lunch, Margie told Caren that Gary wanted to marry her, but she was thinking of breaking off their relationship by summer because she felt hemmed in. Gary always treated her well, but he would check up on her when she was out. She had tried to break up before, but he always talked her out of it.

Margie told Caren that her brother Clifford kept borrowing any money she had in the house, and he didn't always pay it back.

They discussed Margie's dad's cancer, too. Margie worried that one day when she came home from work her father wouldn't be there.

Margie got the train at Suburban Station, but what happened on the other end might have given her pause. When she phoned her dad from Trevose Station around 6 p.m., he didn't answer. No one did.

She must have felt lucky when, just as the sun was setting, she spotted Carole Ebersole, another graduate of Archbishop Wood High School for Girls. Carole, who was at the train station to pick up her father, offered Margie a lift. At about 6:10 p.m., she pulled up in front of the Abt house. On the short ride from the station, Margie mentioned that she wondered why no one had answered the phone at her house. When she saw both her parents' cars in the driveway, she relaxed. Everything seemed normal. She just thanked the Ebersoles for the ride and hopped out. She walked up the river rock driveway in her cork-bottom leather shoes.

Carole's father, who worked at Bell Telephone like Jack Abt, said he briefly considered walking Margie inside, but he was eager to get home because it was his turn to work Saturday that week. Later, he told a *Philadelphia Daily News* reporter that he wondered what would have happened if he had. That story was headlined, "A Friendly Lift—to Death."

The wall phone was ringing when Margie walked through the kitchen door. She picked it up on the fifth ring. The long, coiled cord was so stretched out that it might have reached far enough to allow Margie to keep chatting as she walked into the living room to hang up her coat. The killer was thrown off balance for a few furious seconds. Luckily for him, the call wasn't for her. It was for her sister Kathy. Margie said nine words: "She's not home. I'll have her call you back."

Two people heard those last words. The first was Judy King, the ninth grader on the other end of the line. The second was the killer, who was listening from behind the living room wall. In a heartbeat, he emerged holding a pistol. Margie, the adventurous teen who dreamed of becoming a nurse, had mere seconds.

The last face she ever saw was a waxen one, wearing wire-rimmed glasses and a metal headband about an inch wide.

Even decades later, there would be a persistent rumor that Margie had talked back to her killer. The killer told police she did not. She opened her mouth, but, before she could say a word, he fired a bullet into her cheek.

When she didn't die instantly, the gunman took advantage of the fact that he was ever so slightly taller. He raised his arm and fired a fatal shot into the top of her skull. Then he shoved her down the cellar steps. She landed near her father's corpse.

At around 6:15, Dot Lombardo drove by the Abt place again, this time with her husband Frank. Glancing over at the house, she remarked that it seemed odd that Peggy's car had been joined by her husband's station wagon, but the whole place was still dark.

Inside the dark house, the ringing phone jangled the killer's nerves. As he wiped blood from the kitchen floor for the fifth time, he worried one of the callers might get suspicious and phone the police. Before he could decide whether to go or stay, he heard a knock.

Gary Engle, Margie's strapping boyfriend, was standing at the kitchen door. He stood six feet tall, but the mod platform-soled black shoes he wore that night made him seem even larger.

While he must have looked formidable standing at the door, a friend described Gary as a big, loveable goofball. He was the kind of person who tried to help people, not knock them down, he said. He didn't do drugs much, except sometimes a little pot with Margie.

He had been dealt a bad hand in life. First, he lost the grandfather who raised him. Then, as his beloved grandmother slowly succumbed to cancer, he nursed her and changed her soiled clothing.

He lived alone in a corrugated metal trailer with a worn exterior and two stout, gray propane tanks outside.

Everybody said Gary stuck like glue to Margie. One of Margie's friends said she didn't think he was worthy of Margie, but she did allow his trailer was not too dirty inside for a single man.

That afternoon, Gary washed his delivery truck and left work promptly. He headed for home shortly after 3 p.m. Killing time with his next-door neighbor, Dave Nugent, he spoke mostly about how eager he was to see Margie and celebrate their anniversary. Sometime before 6:30 p.m., he pulled his 11-year-old, medium-blue Chevy Impala in behind Jack's station wagon. He was in the right place at a very bad time.

When his knock at the door went unanswered, Gary could have backed his Impala out of the driveway and circled back later to pick up Margie for dinner. Instead, he opened the kitchen door and walked into harm's way. The killer lurking on the other side of the living room wall had already choreographed his demise.

Before the gunman showed himself, he waited for Gary to reach the exact spot where he had felled Margie 20 minutes earlier. Taking no chances that the much bigger man in the black vinyl jacket might turn the tables on him, the gunman fired at point-blank range. His .22-magnum hollow-point bullet performed exactly according to specifications. It cut through Gary's face and exploded inside his brain, killing him instantly.

Gary had wanted that night to be special. Instead, the thin man was pushing his body down the basement steps where it formed a pile with Margie's and her dad's.

The killer threw a towel over Gary's face and spread a white sheet over his long frame. He tossed a tire on top of the sheet to muddle the view from the kitchen.

★★★

By 7 p.m., there were so many bodies in the basement that the killer rearranged them so an errant leg wouldn't show under the short swinging doors. For some reason, he took time to place random items near their heads—a cookie jar, Peggy's handbag, and 13 quart-sized beer bottles. Then, for the sixth time, he tidied up the kitchen.

Outside, the Abts' chickens were behaving strangely. After Johnny and his friend rounded them up at about 3:45 p.m., something made them fly the coop again sometime between 5 and 6 p.m. At that time, the birds left the property entirely. A neighbor saw them making their way up Fleetwood Avenue en masse.

The gunman lingered several more minutes in the hopes that Michael or Clifford would come home, but the insistent ringing of the phone kept him on edge. He didn't want to chance one of those callers alerting the police and putting him in jeopardy. Besides, in the back of his mind, he was still wondering if those intermittent creaking noises could mean someone was hiding on the second floor of the house.

There were other considerations too. He had not eaten in more than 10 hours.

When the phone rang again around 7 p.m., it was the last straw. It rattled his nerves. Wary of being cornered in the house, he decided to leave with two Abts still alive.

Ironically, the 7 p.m. caller was probably Michael, who wanted to ask his mother to save him some dinner. He phoned home at 7 p.m. and again at 7:15. When he didn't get an answer the second time, he told his friend something must be wrong. He headed home.

The killer's work was finished. After a ten-and-a-half-hour spree, he walked straight out the Abts' rarely used front door sometime after 7:15 p.m. It was a risky move because the house was seated atop a hill at the intersection of two busy streets.

The moon was in a waxing gibbous phase, where it's not quite full but more than 50 percent illuminated, so he removed his wire-rimmed glasses to throw off anyone who might spot him and describe him to a police artist. He left behind no fingerprints, thanks to his colorful gloves.

His victims' automobiles were lined up in the long driveway in the order he killed them—Peggy's yellow Plymouth Duster with the brown vinyl top, her husband's beige '74 Plymouth Satellite station wagon with the roof rack, then Gary's blue, four-door Chevy Impala. Within minutes, they would be joined by Michael's just-purchased turquoise Ford Galaxie 500.

As he crossed the Abts' front lawn around 7:15 p.m. the thin man who had dropped six bodies had no way of knowing that Michael, the Abt he wanted most, was, at that moment, driving toward him.

The killing on Fleetwood Avenue was over. The methodical gunman was ridiculously lucky that two or more of his athletically built victims hadn't walked through the kitchen door together.

As he vanished into the 35-degree night, the executioner had good reason to be happy. He had gotten away with the worst murder in Bucks County history—or at least it seemed like he had at 7:30 p.m. on March 12.

Much later, he would tell people he was sorry about one thing the happened that day. It was not the children's deaths or the fact that his deeds were forever irreversible. It was just that he couldn't stick around long enough to kill the last two Abts—Michael, 21, and Clifford, 23.

He missed Michael by minutes. He didn't know Clifford was in prison until he read it in the Sunday paper.

By the time Patrolman Clee discovered the carnage that he left, the gunman was polishing off a tuna fish sandwich and watching a little television.

After all Clee had been through that Friday, he still drove to the police station late that night to take care of some unfinished business. He released four suspects he had brought in from the roadway squabble earlier in the evening. "I told them, 'You guys are the luckiest guys in the world,'" he said. "I let them go without charging them."

Around 2 a.m., the family that ran the Scottsville Inn on Brownsville Road felt especially lucky when their daughter, Cathy Urban, walked into the tavern. Cathy's mother clutched her chest and said, "Thank God." In the era before cell phones, Cathy had been unaware her mother and stepfather thought she might have been at the Abt house that night. They had heard there were three female victims, and Cathy was Margie Abt's best friend.

Mary Pollock, Cathy's mother, wrote in her journal for March 12: "Abt Family—Mr., Mrs., Margie, her boyfriend Garson Engle, Johnny, Cathy, plus St. Bernard dog discovered murdered. Michael discovered the tragedy. Thank goodness our Cathy was working until 11, or she could have been one of the victims."

CHAPTER 3

Homicide Hal

> Detective Edwards' fellow officers were impressed when he followed the trajectory of one shot and pulled a stray bullet out of an otherwise unimpressive loaf of bread in the kitchen. He took some ribbing: "What were you doing? Making yourself a sandwich?"

While I slept fewer than two miles away, the man who police had been waiting for pulled his red, late-model Ford Mustang onto Fleetwood Avenue about midnight. Dr. Halbert Fillinger was a real-life Quincy eight months before the medical drama of the same name premiered on NBC with actor Jack Klugman playing a nearly infallible medical examiner.

Dr. Fillinger had 600 guns in his personal collection. He had spent 15 years studying terminal ballistics, the science of how a bullet's energy is transferred to a human target. He was a frequent lecturer at the FBI Academy in Quantico, Virginia, a Navy veteran and an Army veteran, and a fellow in forensic pathology at the world-renowned Cleveland Clinic.

A compact man quick to smile, he was known for his lightning-fast wit, his photographic memory, his bountiful energy and his ability to remember the name of nearly every person he met.

Unlike Klugman's preening Quincy character, Dr. Fillinger's down-to-earth manner belied the fact that he was the forensics expert who would go on to perform the autopsies on Yippee leader Abbie Hoffman following his suicide, on NBC anchor Jessica Savitch after she drowned in her car, and on U.S. Senator H. John Heinz III, the ketchup-family scion who died when his small plane collided with a helicopter over an elementary school playground.

Off the job, Dr. Fillinger was a light-hearted regular guy who restored antique firetrucks as a hobby and wasn't above an occasional spoof phone call. He eventually added a vanity plate to his car as a joke: It read Hom Hal, short for Homicide Hal.

On the job, he was a note-perfect professional. He was generous with his time and knowledge. He'd say "use me" to nurses, reporters, paramedics, firefighters, and police officers. He meant they should use his knowledge; call him any time if they had a question. He made time for everyone. It was not unusual for him to work through the night.

When I heard Dr. Fillinger had been in the Abts' basement Friday night, I regretted leaving the scene even more. He had always been a great source for reporters. He loved his work, and he loved talking about it. He invited me to sit in on an autopsy in Philadelphia once. The stench from one decomposing body was stomach-churning, even in the large, well-ventilated morgue, but listening to him dictate notes into a hanging microphone as he weighed the organs was more educational than any science course I took.

It was after midnight on Friday when he entered the Abt house by the basement door. Lieutenant Zajac followed right behind him. What they found there was a grotesque tableau of six fully clothed corpses, all shot in the face.

Bodies were strewn from one end of the basement to the other. There was no sign any of them put up a struggle. The place was not ransacked. Nothing was taken. There was no sign of sexual assault. Several were still wearing their winter coats. The detectives had a terrifying mystery to solve.

It was a shambles in the 16th-century use of the word, when a shambles was a scene of loathsome slaughter. "It was hard to believe," Lieutenant Zajac told reporters later. "Six people killed. Just lying down there."

Police officers followed in Dr. Fillinger's footsteps, but it wasn't easy. The basement was a jumble of standard cellar staples like tools and a bicycle and a sawhorse. The clutter wasn't what made the officers' jobs knotty, though. Every few feet, they came upon a corpse with its face thrashed with hollow-point bullets. Two of them were children.

It was a grim task, especially for detectives who had children of their own. County Detective Richard Batezel had six. Lieutenant Zajac had three—an 8-year-old, a 10-year-old and one Kathy's age. "You think, Christ, how can somebody commit a crime against a kid that age," Zajac said later.

Detective Eckert had seen small children killed in auto accidents, and he thought he was jaded to that kind of thing until he saw the Abt bodies.

District Attorney Ken Biehn said one harrowing thought crossed all the men's minds—an outsider had somehow invaded a family home.

Jack Abt lay face up at the bottom of the wooden steps. His car keys lay nearby. His blood pooled on the cement below.

Margie, who made the lethal mistake of not noticing anything in the few seconds when she was talking on the phone in the kitchen, lay near the steps, too. Dr. Fillinger determined her mouth was open when she was shot at extremely close range. When the muzzle of a gun is held close to a victim, the explosion of gunpowder that pushes the bullet out can cause tattooing—reddish flecks similar to cinders imbedded in the skin. Scarlet tattooing pierced Margie's face from her forehead to her chin. It outlined her lips and dotted the inside of her mouth.

Her boyfriend, Gary, who was looking forward to taking her to dinner that night, landed in the same area 20 minutes after she did. A single hollow-point bullet ripped through his left cheek, pierced his brain and shattered his spinal column.

In his report to the district attorney, Dr. Fillinger described the bodies of Jack, Margie and Gary as "tumbled together" at the bottom of the stairs.

The killer fired just one bullet into Johnny's left cheek, but it mushroomed inside his head and neck. The gun barrel was so close to his head that the tattooing it left mimicked a strawberry birthmark stretching from his eyebrow to his chin.

Peggy lay near her two youngest children. Four gunshots had riddled her face.

Twelve-year-old Kathy had been shot in her face three times.

By the time Dr. Fillinger arrived, rigor mortis, a temporary stiffening of the muscles, had set in on Johnny's body, which the killer had dragged to a spot near the furnace. Heat hastens the tautening. The other bodies were just beginning to go into rigor when Dr. Fillinger examined them around 12:30 a.m.

Heidi, the old Saint Bernard, lay next to the door with a jacket thrown across her ample midsection. She had bled to death.

The shooter left a substantial amount of money in his victim's wallets and purses, a sure sign he wasn't there to rob.

Police began dusting for fingerprints at the basement door. Before the weekend was over, they had lifted prints from automobiles, coffee cups, faucet handles, window sashes, the phone book, a Saltines box, a pack of Winstons and several quart bottles of Ballantine beer. It was an evidence technician's worst nightmare—a household with fingerprints from seven family members, all their visitors and maybe their killer.

As the officers moved agonizingly slowly from the back door in, they picked up an enormous amount of evidence. The problem, as one of them explained, is you really don't know what you're looking for.

Detective Bill Edwards, the department's evidence technician, photographed every room in the house from several angles. One shot showed a narcotics pipe. One focused on some unidentified seeds. One showed a wallet-sized, plasticized prayer card sticking up from behind the thermostat in the living room. It featured a drawing of Jesus with his hands outstretched and these words: "Heavenly Father, Almighty God, we humbly beseech Thee to bless and sanctify this house and all who dwell therein." It is not known whether the killer read it.

Police recovered bullet fragments from the living room, the hallway, the bathroom and from a loaf of bread in the kitchen. Projectiles roosted in items of furniture, stairs, doorframes and the linoleum floor. They came to rest in an ashtray, in a wooden stool, in front of the refrigerator, below the wall phone, under the kitchen hutch, in front of the color television set and under a beige leather chair in the living room. One of Heidi's teeth lay next to a rocking chair. A stray bullet chipped the toilet bowl in the bathroom at the top of the living room stairs. Police found another in the bathtub.

Detective Edwards spent days painstakingly mapping the bullets' paths. "He was like living over there," one detective said.

Edwards' fellow officers were impressed when he followed the trajectory of one shot and pulled a stray bullet out of that otherwise unimpressive loaf of bread in the kitchen. He took some ribbing: "What were you doing? Making yourself a sandwich?"

Edwards didn't usually talk much about his work at home, but he did tell his wife, Lucy, about his find that night. "Who else would ever think to check the bread?" she said decades later. "That's how thorough he was. He would even check the bread. He loved his work!"

Edwards was a perfectionist and a trained professional, but much of what any detective knows is learned case-by-case on the job. That was true for him, too. After collecting pubic hairs for one case, he placed his tiny finds in an envelope. He made the mistake of licking the flap to seal it. Other officers found it uproariously funny. After that, Edwards went to a stationery store and bought a sponge-topped envelope moistener.

Detectives moved slowly and deliberately to bag as much evidence as possible. There's no clue too small to interest crime scene investigators. Edmond Locard, a 19th-century French criminologist known as the Sherlock Holmes of France, came up with Locard's Principle of Exchange in 1910. The nut of it is every criminal will bring something to the crime scene and leave with something from it. So, when a promising piece of material was discovered on a doorway, hopes were raised until it turned out to be threads from something a detective was wearing.

The killer did leave one thing that could possibly help nab him later. While he was maneuvering bodies around the basement, he left a size-9D boot print in blood.

The crime scene was alarming for police, especially for officers like Dechant and Clee and Eckert, who grew up in Trevose. "It was really unsettling having that many people killed," Eckert remembered. "That was something you just didn't see."

When Dave Clee had time to think about everything that happened that extraordinary night, he wondered why Michael didn't check the basement before he ran outside to ask the neighbors if they had seen his family.

"I don't know why he didn't see those bodies," Clee said. "To this day, I don't know why he didn't look."

CHAPTER 4

What the Hell is Going on Here?

When a dog barked in Trevose, people looked out their windows to see why.

The roller-coaster investigation of the Abt murders began with Officer Clee's grim discovery. It would end with an arrest that would surprise nearly everyone.

In the 10 days separating those events, homeowners who never locked their doors at night searched for their keys. They put timers on their lights. When a dog barked in Trevose, people looked out their windows to see why.

As Chief Michaels put it, "People are asking what the hell is loose here." One officer assigned to guard the inside of the Abt house was wondering the same thing.

George Berry, a muscular, tattooed sergeant who was a top scorer on the police aptitude test, wasn't happy that he drew the housesitting assignment. He did spend one night inside the murder scene, though. Even years later, he said it was the worst feeling he ever had in his life, just strange beyond belief. He told his wife Paige that the officers assigned to stay overnight heard moans, footsteps, and doors slamming. He called it "bone-chilling." He thought the place was haunted.

Other police officers said it would take a lot to spook Sergeant Berry, who carried a bowie knife in addition to his service revolver, and, sometimes, a few extra weapons. He was a legend within the department. The tall, deep-voiced sergeant once walked into the police station holding an angry snapping turtle by the tail. One day he gave a fat, 66-inch-long boa constrictor a ride in his patrol car, and he bought a mouse for the snake to snack on en route. "We called him Crazy George," one patrolman reminisced. "He was a great guy, but he was a scary guy."

Sergeant Berry was a force at donkey basketball, a game where players ride live donkeys across the court to score and raise money for local charities. While other police officers and township paramedics dragged their stubborn donkeys behind them to get in position to score, he stationed himself under the basket on an immobile donkey and scored 16 of the winning police team's 20 points.

★★★

The Abt slayings shocked even seasoned law enforcement because they deviated from other mass shootings in '70s America in a key way. The killer had lain in wait inside the home of a loving and devoted family. Shattering the sanctity of a home was a rare and chilling phenomenon in 1976. Home is where people feel most protected, so a shooter invading that space was harrowing.

Most mass murders up until then were one-off slayings like the sharpshooter who set up a sniper's nest in the University of Texas clock tower in 1966, and the killer who opened fire at a downtown Howard Johnson's in New Orleans in 1973.

Dennis Rader, the self-proclaimed BTK killer who terrorized Wichita, Kansas, did lie in wait for one of his victims in 1974, but, overwhelmingly, when a person was executed inside his home in the '70s, it was the work of a family member.

And, even then, when John List killed five members of his family at his New Jersey home in 1971, his crime was so unthinkable that it furnished the inspiration for a podcast, three films, a Netflix miniseries, episodes of *Law & Order* and *American Justice* and an exhibit at the National Museum of Crime & Punishment in Washington, D.C.

And, when Ronald DeFeo Jr. shot his parents and four siblings in their Long Island home in 1974, his actions were so shocking that they became the basis for several books and dozens of movies, including *The Amityville Horror*, the highest-grossing independent film of all time until the 1990s.

★★★

Mass murder was so rare in America in the '70s that many people in Trevose had a tough time putting it into words.

One woman rushed the words out. Some neighbors referred to it only as "it." Some called it "what happened to the Abts." It was a truly unspeakable crime.

Clifford usually referred to the slayings as "this thing that happened."

Michael called it "it" or "this" or "what happened to my family."

One woman said she got goosebumps whenever she told someone what happened to the Abts.

After Maria D'Ambrosio's mother picked her up at roller skating that Friday night, she asked her if she noticed anything funny at the Abt house when she went to collect for the *Courier Times*. The papergirl said she didn't. At a loss for words to describe such an unprecedented and horrific event, Mrs. D'Ambrosio blurted out, "Well, they were all killed."

"You just couldn't believe it," Maryann Zebrowski McGinnis of Trevose remembered. "Back then, you didn't have that kind of stuff."

Ruth Hallas, who lived two blocks from the Abts, was floored when she heard the entire family had been killed, even the children. "I can't even cry," she said. "I'm in such a state of shock. Those were such nice kids."

The Hallases' own 15-year-old daughter had been killed in a freak accident on Fleetwood Avenue nine months earlier when an antique gun fired unexpectedly, but Mrs. Hallas said the Abt murders seemed like something out of *In Cold Blood*, the Truman Capote bestseller about the robbery-murder of a prominent Kansas family in 1959.

Echoing her later, a *Philadelphia Bulletin* headline asked, "Why Was the Abt Family Killed?" The story described the children as "well-mannered" and the parents as "concerned." The Bulletin reporter picked up early on the one thing that detracted from the picture of the Abts as the all-American family: "Except for the fact that one son was in jail, they seemed like a typical, middle class, suburban Bucks County family."

That one glaring exception would pull investigators into a 10-day wild goose chase.

CHAPTER 5

Bollixed Lives

People wondered why not one of the Abts' neighbors heard a shot all day when at least 17 bullets were fired. The police chief pointed out that the house was well-built, and the nearest neighbor was nearly 100 feet away. Soon Dr. Fillinger would come upon the real reason, which was much more gruesome.

Clifford Abt's future was abruptly scrambled on Saturday morning, March 13. Instead of the expected jailhouse visit from his mom and his fiancée, he was being told that his mother, father, brother and two sisters were gone forever, along with his sister's boyfriend. He and his brother Michael were all that was left of their family of seven. The details were still sketchy.

Clifford phoned his fiancée, Shelly Robbins, who had been expected for dinner at the Abt house Friday night. She told Clifford she skipped it because she didn't feel up to the drive from Philadelphia. Then he told her his woeful news. Days later, Shelly's story would hit the newspapers with the headline: "Shelly Robbins Missed Appointment with Death."

Minutes after Shelly and Clifford hung up, her mother returned from a dental appointment with a throbbing mouth. She asked matter-of-factly if Peg had phoned yet about their planned road trip to the prison. They had expected a call Friday night, but it never came. Shelly told her mother the preposterous news.

Michael Abt's Saturday morphed like his brother's. He had planned to serve as best man at his friend's wedding that day. Instead, he was helping plan his family's mass funeral.

Michael Abt and his childhood friend Ed Allahand experienced an unexpected role reversal that defied all odds. When Allahand's mother had died suddenly on February 23, Michael came by to console him and take him out drinking in New Jersey. Not even three weeks later, things boomeranged. By mid-March, it was Allahand who was consoling Michael about his mother's sudden death.

★★★

Several hundred people's Saturdays had been disordered by one heart-breaking event.

Philadelphia Police Detective Bill Haney, Peggy's brother who had been working in the mobile police van on her front lawn late Friday night, woke before 6 a.m. to meet his brother at his widowed mother's home so they could deliver the tragic news about their sister and her family before their mother heard it on the radio.

Fleetwood Avenue was buzzing at sunup Saturday morning despite an on-again, off-again drizzle. Police were at work inside and outside the house. They temporarily impounded the four cars parked in a row in the driveway. Two officers with pipes dangling out of their mouths bent to pour wet plaster into a deep footprint left near a window. Detective Edwards bagged evidence in the bloody basement. An officer strung a thick hemp rope around the front yard and propped a "Keep Out" sign next to a bush.

Four men carried Heidi's blood-caked carcass out the basement door for delivery to the University of Pennsylvania Veterinary Hospital for a necropsy. Bill Fox, who was holding one end of the tarp, guessed she weighed about 170 pounds. The long-haired Saint Bernard had been very active until about two years earlier. More recently, she spent her days napping on the second floor after her family members left for the day.

At John and Dorothy Mitchell's house down the street from the Abts, the phone kept ringing that Saturday morning, even more than usual in a house with five children. It turned out several friends and relatives had just heard a snippet of the television news report that a family on

Fleetwood Avenue had been murdered, the father's name was John and the couple had five children.

A dispatcher on duty at the police station that morning took a call from a man named Chuck Engle, who heard the news on the radio and wanted more information. He was Gary's uncle.

Neighborhood kids knotted in front of the Abts' driveway. Several sported Flyers gear. The city's NHL expansion team had won the Stanley Cup two years running, and fans were hopeful. Adult neighbors, even a few who seldom mixed with others, milled around and traded information about the murders. A couple talked to the news reporters roving the block.

***

Letter carrier William Strange, back on his route that morning, placed a single envelope in the Abts' mailbox. It was their annual county tax bill.

The mailman knew that Jack would have had only months to live if he hadn't been shot. Peggy had told him. He thought Jack looked good the last time he saw him.

***

When a television crew asked Officer Clee his reaction to the slayings on his own street, the patrolman who found the bodies gave the standard answer neighbors always give: You expect this kind of thing to happen far away in Texas or California, but you don't expect it to happen in your own neighborhood.

A television viewer in Texas saw the news clip and mailed letters of complaint to the police chief and to Pennsylvania Governor Milton J. Shapp. Clee's remarks maligned her native state, she said. She wanted Clee reprimanded, and she expected apologies from him, Chief Michaels and the governor.

Clee wrote her a letter reminding her that Texas was the location of the 1966 University of Texas tower shooting, then the deadliest mass shooting by a lone gunman in U.S. history. He threw in the mostly fictional Texas Chain Saw Massacre. And he wound it up with, "Remember the Alamo."

At his superior officers' suggestion, he never mailed it. He still has it though.

***

Dr. Fillinger was with Gary Engle and the Abts again Saturday evening, but this time they were at the Lower Bucks County Hospital morgue. He arrived at 8 p.m. to begin the six autopsies, but Bensalem Detectives Ed Keyser and Tom Scaricaciottoli and Bucks County Detective John Wagner had been prepping the bodies since mid-afternoon.

It was Detective Keyser's first autopsy. He put Vaseline in his nostrils and smoked a cigar—two standard methods to mask any whiffs of putrescine and cadaverine, the foul-smelling compounds in corpses. I couldn't get through one autopsy as an observer sitting at the far end of a big room. He made it through six as an active participant.

They tagged the bodies "H1" through "H6"—Jack Abt through Kathy Abt. They undressed the victims and bagged and tagged all their clothing. Hair samples were taken as evidence. Detective Wagner took photos. A radiologist took X-rays of the six cadavers, beginning with Jack.

As Dr. Fillinger removed all the bullets, the detectives bagged them for delivery to the FBI lab in Washington, D.C.

They worked long enough that they ordered food, which they ate outside in the corridor.

The six autopsy reports sent to the district attorney all listed the same cause and manner of death. Cause: Gunshot wounds of the head. Manner: Homicide.

Dr. Fillinger's postmortem explained why none of the neighbors heard a thing. All the victims were shot at such close range that their bodies acted as silencers, absorbing the loud "bang" sound.

***

The Abt murder story ran in newspapers from Hackensack, New Jersey, to Honolulu, Hawaii that weekend. The *New York Times* made room on page 40 of its Sunday edition for five paragraphs headlined: "Six Killed in Home Near Philadelphia." The *Philadelphia Inquirer* topped its story with the daunting head: "Slayer of Six Hunted in Suburb: Family is Found in Cellar." The *Odessa American* in Odessa, Texas, laid the mass homicide news over two columns. It didn't quite cover the columns evenly, so someone filled in the extra inch with a random joke.

While newspaper subscribers were still learning the chilling details of the murders over their morning coffee, volunteer firefighters in full uniform were already at work emptying the frigid, green water from the bulging above-ground swimming pool that covered most of the Abts' backyard. Police officers stared into the big blue oval as the water went out. They hoped to spot a gun or ammunition at the murky bottom.

They found no weapons or clues there, just several inches of browned leaves and a few items that gave Bob Hickey pause. Hickey, a 23-year-old volunteer with the Trevose Fire Company, was saddened when he spotted balls and toys in the water. He stood just yards from the basement door Kathy's and Johnny's bodies were carried through one day earlier. "It was an eerie feeling," Hickey said. "You knew that right through that door six people died. Six murders a mile from the firehouse."

The firefighters also emptied the small decorative fountain next to the spot on the front lawn where Jack liked to spread his lawn chair and read his afternoon papers when the weather was right. There was no evidence there, either.

***

Dr. John McGrath's necropsy determined Heidi's cause of death to be bullet wounds of the head and abdomen. When the huge Saint Bernard raced down the stairs to protect her family, the terrified gunman shot her six times.

Heidi's death was a sad addendum to the Abt slayings. Hearts sank as newspaper readers learned the killer or killers had taken the life of a

Saint Bernard, one of the most beloved dog breeds, one known for its loyalty and playfulness.

★★★

The executive editor at my paper wasn't happy with me that Saturday morning because I didn't give anyone a heads up about six murders on my beat. I didn't know there were six victims. Neither did the Philadelphia reporters. Somehow, Robert Marek, a reporter for the *Courier Post*, 20 miles away and across the state line in Cherry Hill, New Jersey, got all the details on Friday night. He wrote an excellent story for his Saturday paper, and his editors put it on the AP wire, a news-sharing nonprofit that supplies stories to papers and broadcast stations around the country.

By the time I woke up Saturday, the news of the Abt killings was blaring from the local radio channels and Philadelphia television stations.

I thought it would be best not to mention that I had been sitting in front of the crime scene 90 minutes after the bodies were discovered. The editor was upset, but good editors always come up with a backup plan, and there was also an it-is-what-it-is attitude. Since we had no Saturday edition, he knew we couldn't publish a story until Sunday anyway.

He concentrated on getting the best coverage we could for our next edition. Ten reporters were assigned to gather facts that Saturday. We were like miners hoping to find a vein of coal or archeologists trying to uncover some ancient shards. If we found enough lumps and shards, we'd have a readable package of news and features for the Sunday paper.

The fact that some of the newsmen had never been to Trevose didn't matter. Reporters often parachute into events with no names or contacts except whatever they can scare up in minutes.

In the '70s, before the internet, that meant dashing into the newsroom library and searching alphabetically for old stories in "the clips"—tiny brown envelopes labeled "Bensalem police" and "John Abt" and "Trevose."

Before databases and search engines and desktop computers, we relied on the clips that librarians with scissors cut from each day's newspaper and folded until they fit into manila envelopes just a little larger than an index card. Thousands of alphabetized brown envelopes filled dozens of gray filing cabinets, each envelope with a typewritten title in its upper-right-hand corner—"Homicides 1970" or "Crime Statistics" or "Zajac, Theodore R. Jr."

You'd glean all the information you could from the clips, check a map, get to the scene and ask questions until you can answer at least the five basic questions readers always have—what happened, who did it happen to, when did it happen, where did it happen and why did it happen. The why often took more time.

★★★

The Bensalem Township Police Department was just 25 years old in 1976. Born in 1951 with one officer, one chief and one patrol car, it was continually expanding to keep up with a building boom. The township was fast becoming a commuter suburb of Philadelphia. Keystone Racetrack rose out of a field there in 1974. Strip shopping centers popped up. The upscale 1-million-square-foot Neshaminy Mall opened in 1963, distinguished by the five-story totem pole in the parking lot, a nod to the Lenni Lenape tribe who once inhabited the land.

When Pat and Ted Zajac were married in 1964, police officers were required to live in the township, but the newlyweds could not find a single garden apartment available for rent there. They wound up living in an apartment over a hardware store until they could buy their first house. Just 10 years later, newly installed pipes were bringing water and sewers to thousands of new garden apartments, and more were on the way.

The police force was growing too, with 29 officers by the early '70s, and many of them were taking advanced training to become specialists.

But, in March 1976, there were still fewer than 10 detectives to solve the largest murder mystery in Bucks County history.

Police in television crime shows solve cases with DNA, street cameras, credit card records, cell tower pings and facial-recognition software. The officers knocking on doors in the darkness in Trevose that Friday evening had none of those tools. The first use of DNA in a criminal case was 11 years off.

Bensalem officers didn't know if they were searching for one killer or more. They had no idea whether the killer or killers were local or if they arrived via one of the four major highways that crisscross in Bensalem—U.S. Route 1, the Pennsylvania Turnpike, then unfinished I-95 and busy five-lane Street Road. The turnpike, which could carry a driver to the Ohio state line, was just two and a half miles from the murder scene.

★★★

On Saturday, Chief Michaels updated reporters: "No suspects, no arrests, no weapon and no motive." A murder-suicide was ruled out because no gun was found near the bodies.

People wondered why not one of the Abts' neighbors heard a shot all day when at least 17 bullets were fired. The chief pointed out that the house was well-built, and the nearest neighbor was nearly 100 feet away. Soon Dr. Fillinger would come upon the real reason, which was much more gruesome.

★★★

The chief pronounced the killer either a "wacko" or a "cold-blooded killer." "A normal person cannot sustain emotional heat long enough to kill an entire family unless he's crazy or a cold-blooded killer," he said.

Asked if he thought it was a professional hit, he said the killers were very cruel, but he didn't know about professional.

With more questions than answers, the chief started riffing. He said his personal feeling was the killer or killers were not acquainted with the Abts. He based his opinion on a "gut feeling" that someone who knew the family would not have killed the dog.

When he went on to compare the Abt murders to the Charlie Manson slayings that rocked Los Angeles in 1969, reporters started scribbling furiously in their coil-topped notebooks again.

No one, of course, had the answer to the question in the back of everyone's mind: Would the killer or killers strike again as the Manson family did in Los Angeles the next night?

The headline in the Sunday *Courier Times* was: "County's Worst Mass Murder Leaves Police with Few Leads and No Motive."

Readers who flipped to page 12 saw an odd, random headline: "Next Rotary President may be Ex-Nazi: Lower Bucks Rotarians are Concerned."

CHAPTER 6

Two More Victims

> She was fully dressed and she had a book open on her lap. From where he was standing, he thought she was asleep.

Readers reeling from the mass murder news in the Sunday papers were stunned again when they picked up their Monday papers. The banner headline stripped across the front page read: "Langhorne Couple Tortured and Murdered: Rare Taser Gun Shocked Victims Before Killings."

Oddly, it happened during the same hours the Abts were killed and only four miles away.

Someone terrorized two 77-year-olds with an electric stun gun and then shot them execution style. It happened in the sitting room of a graceful Victorian farmhouse in Langhorne, an historic borough with Quaker roots dating back to 1680. Because the couple lived alone, the grisly murders weren't discovered until Sunday.

Neighbors gathering behind the yellow police tape that night buzzed that they had suspected something was up at Ed and Marguerite Vogenberger's place all weekend because every light in the house was on. The Vogenbergers were so frugal they made a habit of keeping only one light on at a time.

A fully lit house was so unusual that it caused one passerby to phone the switchboard at Trevose State Police Barracks on Saturday. A trooper did a drive-by of the brick farmhouse nestled in a stand of trees, but he noticed nothing out of the ordinary and went on his way. He didn't spot the Friday afternoon newspaper still folded on the front step.

Then, on Sunday, Middletown Township Detective Donald Mather drove to the farm on other business. When he pulled onto the Vogenberger property, his car rolled over a traffic hose Ed Vogenberger kept stretched across his wide driveway. The hose tripped a bell that alerted the Vogenbergers that a customer was arriving at the farm stand where they sold their corn, beans and tomatoes. The hose worked the same way gas station bells did in the 1950s. The ringing usually caused one of the Vogenbergers to appear in the driveway. That day no one came.

Mather noticed the back door to the house was wide open despite temperatures in the 40s. He could hear the loud television from the yard. It was tuned to Action News. He rang the doorbell but got no answer. He peered through a window and spotted Marguerite Vogenberger in her rocking chair in the sitting room. She was fully dressed and she had a book open on her lap. From where he was standing, he thought she was asleep. Her husband of 57 years lay on a couch nearby, clad in a grey work shirt and brown pants.

Mather, who had known the Vogenbergers since he was a kid, leaned in for a closer look. That's when he spotted the blood. He entered the house and came upon a curious crime scene, every bit as alarming as the Abts' house.

As he approached Marguerite Vogenberger's rocker, he saw a copy of James A. Mitchener's *Centennial* propped open in her lap. Blood from her nose had turned her green kitchen apron red all the way to her waist. An odd, loose wire was sticking out of her stomach. Another thin wire dangled from her left leg.

Her husband, Ed, was lying on his stomach, half on and half off the bloody couch. He had two unexplained holes in the back of his shirt. His pants rode up several inches above the tops of his socks, as if he had been struggling to roll off the couch and stand up.

Police learned the thin wires and pierced clothing were leftovers from agonizing jolts with a Taser, an electronic stun gun that had been on the market for about a year. Tasers fire electric darts capable of immobilizing even a young, healthy individual. One dart can disrupt the nervous system for about 15 minutes. And, once a dart hits a victim, more shocks can be inflicted through a thin wire that connects the dart to the gun.

Marguerite's killer hadn't even bothered to remove his wires from her body.

"I just couldn't believe what I was seeing was actually there," Mather said.

Nearly echoing Lieutenant Zajac's reaction to the Abt bodies, Mather later told reporters it was hard to even imagine that someone would do what he saw before him.

The small, fading, full-color crime-scene photos evoke thoughts of a shoebox diorama of a typical 1970s living room. The couple's earth-toned sitting room was punctuated with crocheted doilies, Sears catalogs, heavy glass ashtrays, well-thumbed telephone books, bright-yellow *National Geographics* and the previous night's *Courier Times* neatly folded to page C-36—the television schedule. The prime-time lineup started with two hit shows—*The Waltons* and *Welcome Back, Kotter.*

The first floor of the farmhouse was largely undisturbed except for a purse on the kitchen table. Its contents were strewn across the table. The upstairs was a different story. As Police Chief Howard Shook put it, "It was ransacked something terrible."

Detective Mather figured the thieves tortured the Vogenbergers with Tasers to persuade them to divulge where they kept their cash. When the couple wouldn't give it up, the robbers overturned shoe boxes and tossed dresser drawers and emptied closets in a frenzied search.

Then, before they left, they shot Marguerite once in the back of the head and her husband twice in the temple. It was unclear whether the robbers killed the couple to avoid being identified or out of frustration because they couldn't find any valuables.

Police didn't know what was taken because they didn't know what the victims had.

James Hudson, Ed Vogenberger's friend and neighbor for 38 years, told a reporter the Vogenbergers were plain, good old-fashioned people who kept to themselves. They worked all summer and, in the winter, they would travel to Florida or California and never tell anybody they were leaving.

The day after the bodies were discovered, headlines blared the bizarre news: "Darts Blamed in Slayings" and "Bucks Couple Stun-Tortured."

Chief Shook sat down with *Courier Times* reporter Bill Newill to explain how the Tasers worked, but the compact gray guns were so new that the chief didn't have one to show him. When Newill phoned the newsroom to dictate his story on the double murder, he included an explanation of how the new weapon worked. He told the rewrite man the couple was tortured with "something called a Taser, which is something like an electric gun." The voice on the other end of the line asked, "Like a cattle prod?" "No," Newill answered. "Apparently, you just hold it in your hand. It's not that big."

***

Jack Cover, a NASA engineer who worked on the moon landing, came up with the idea for the Taser after he read about a man who had walked into an electrified fence and was only temporarily stunned. He thought he could use the same technology to cook up a weapon that federal air marshals could wield against airline hijackers. Cover took to his garage to create a gun that would fire electronic darts instead of bullets that could damage a plane's fuselage.

At just over nine inches long, the new weapon looked more like a heavy-duty rectangular flashlight than a gun. Cover named it the Taser—an acronym for his favorite childhood book about the adventures of a boy and his rifle that shoots bolts of electricity. The book title was *Tom Swift and his Electric Rifle*, but Cover added the "A" to make the name easier to pronounce.

When the airlines opted for pat-downs and metal detectors instead, Cover began marketing his $200 stun guns to police and private citizens. Of the 3,500 sold in the first few months, only about 100 of them went to police officers. Criminals swiftly caught on to the Taser's usefulness.

***

Although the Abt and Vogenberger crime scenes were just five miles apart, the Vogenbergers' farm was in the Middletown Township police district. The Abts' Trevose home was patrolled by Bensalem Township police.

Detectives thought the murders were probably not linked, but officers timed the drive between the crime scenes at different hours, gauging how long it would take a killer to travel from one murder house to the other. At one time of day, it took them eight minutes. At another, four minutes and 20 seconds.

Normally, any murder in quaint Langhorne Borough would have left county residents shaken. Two multiple murders four miles apart gave even seasoned detectives a sense of unease.

"Those two incidents happening together really gave you pause," Detective Eckert said. "For a second. we thought, 'Holy God, could these actually be connected?'"

***

Reporters thrive on breaking news, the bigger the headline the better, but the news that two 77-year-olds were tortured with an electric stun gun put everyone on edge. Nerves were still jangled from the previous day's news about six people murdered by a man who leaped out from behind a living room wall.

Reporters have beats like waitresses have tables. We are on the hook to serve up any news that happens on our beats, but we are also on guard against pushy reporters who try to poach good stories from our beats. Beats were sort of suspended that March. There was an all-hands-on-deck state of mind. Reporters who couldn't have pointed out Trevose on a map a week earlier were knocking on doors up and down Fleetwood Avenue. They rushed in all directions to cover four or five angles on each murder and still keep up with other breaking news. The mood in the newsroom was intense, as it always was when there was a big story, but this news seemed jolting. Everybody around the city desk was talking about it. It was a double mystery. Eight people had been murdered, and their killers had vanished into thin air.

Carl La Vo, a news reporter, was surprised by the diabolical nature of the crimes. He, too, thought it seemed like *In Cold Blood* in lovely Bucks County.

Ellie Reader, a copy editor, drove through Langhorne on her way to work. Spotting the sign for the Vogenbergers' street would bring to mind what happened there. "Langhorne was this tidy, little Victorian town that looked stuck in the 19th century," she said. "I couldn't imagine anything like a double murder happening there."

Phil Weck, the paper's editorial editor, personally relayed the latest news on the murders to local Rotarians every Wednesday. Weck looked every inch the classic newspaper editor with his impish smile, thinning white hair, black plastic spectacles and gentlemanly dress complete with narrow ties, shirts that were always just a little too roomy, hand-knit vests, pleated dress pants and well-shined shoes. To young reporters, he was a genial mentor.

In the 1950s, he had reported for United Press International, one of the largest newswire services in the world. In the '60s, he was editor of *Official Detective Stories*, a racy crime magazine with headlines like "Who Butchered the Marine in the Pink Nightie?" and "Terrible Revenge of the Nympho's Spurned Lover." In the '70s, his quick wit and his award-winning writing made him a local celebrity in Bucks County.

Members of the Rotary Club of Bristol looked forward to the "newscasts" Weck delivered at their weekly lunch meetings at the Bristol Motor Inn. He dished on everything from murder investigations to tax increases. Afterwards, he would take questions from members.

★★★

Dr. Fillinger had spent most of his weekend working the Abt murders in Trevose, but he returned to Bucks County on Monday night. This time he was with the Vogenbergers. Although their bodies weren't discovered until Sunday, his examinations determined they were killed on Friday during the same late afternoon and early evening hours as the Abts.

A *Courier Times* editorial called it a "weekend of horror." All citizens were urged to supply investigators with whatever information they might have.

After the news of the torture deaths hit the newspapers, a baseless rumor circulated that a Taser gun was found in the Abts' basement too. Michael Abt denied it. So did the police.

Police officers fanned out to 11 stores in three states, searching for the one that sold the Taser used to torture the Vogenbergers.

The writer of the "Good Evening" column that anchored the front page of the *Courier Times* switched a few words around in the old adage that trouble comes in threes. He tailored it to fit the local news: "It may be an old wives' tale, but trouble does seem to come in bunches. No sooner did Bucks County discover six dead in one family than two more murdered persons were found in Langhorne ..."

The column of quips and questions ran on the *Courier Times*' front page every day, but not everyone at the paper was a fan. Joe Gross, an irreverent sportswriter miffed because he was required to wear a tie to work, once walked into the newsroom wearing a shiny oversized clown tie over a white undershirt on which he had drawn a color caricature of the columnist and oversized letters that spelled out, "Good Evening."

After news of the double murder broke, police dispatchers took calls from employees at several banks. They all wanted to report that the Vogenbergers had deposited money or stock certificates with their institutions.

Detective Mather, who became lead on the Vogenberger case, suspected a shirttail cousin of Marguerite Vogenberger was the doer. Francis "Gator" Tomlinson had been serving time for rape and murder at Graterford Prison until six months earlier when he managed to scale the 30-foot rock walls using a handmade rope. He was on the run with an armed robber named John Dickel, and they had been spotted in Bucks County. Tomlinson had burgled the farmhouse once before, and Detective Mather thought he might have returned.

The sole eyewitness in the case was Arthur Krauss, a neighbor who saw a dark-haired man leaving the farm early Sunday morning carrying a potato basket full of clothing. Krauss didn't think anything of it because the Vogenbergers often hired men to work the farm, but, when he saw the mobile crime van 10 hours later, he thought the man might have been up to no good.

Mather sent more than 100 items from the farmhouse to the FBI labs in Washington, D.C., but neither man's prints were found on any of them. He had only one item that might link the duo to the farm—a rippled-sole boot print left in the dust in the attic. Oddly, the dusty boot print in the Vogenbergers' attic was identical to the bloody one in the Abts' basement.

Lock sales exploded in Langhorne Borough and Middletown Township that week.

CHAPTER 7

The Killer is Behind You

> One officer joked, "One of these days we're going to find somebody standing stark naked at Gino's preaching the gospel, and that will be our boy."

A cold, windy Monday morning was made worse for workers at the IRS Philadelphia office as they lamented Peggy Abt's murder. Someone took up a collection for her boys. They also filed paperwork to give her survivors the $26,000 payout on her government life insurance. It was $13,000 more than the face value because her murder triggered double indemnity. The sons would receive a payout of her federal pension benefits, too.

***

Television news trucks swept onto Fleetwood Avenue again Monday morning. Journalists interviewed anyone who knew an Abt. The Abts' 19-year-old next-door neighbor Bruce Tomlinson told a newsman he didn't think whoever did it would come back. "He had it in for them," he said. "He was not just some nut running around."

Most neighbors told the roving reporters the Abts were "nice" and "quiet," but not one neighbor to the rear. She told a reporter they were "anything but quiet." She called Peggy Abt "outspoken" and said the family was "a puzzle" with cars coming and going from their house all the time. She said she planted bushes so she wouldn't have to see them, at least not in the summertime.

Her remarks seemed harsh on the heels of Peggy Abt's horrific murder, but a different neighbor said the Abt boys bullied the neighbor to the rear's sons so relentlessly that she drove them to school daily for years so they wouldn't have to wait for the bus with the Abts. They rode their bikes up and down their own short driveway to avoid encountering the Abt boys on a ride around the block, he said.

★★★

When police drove Michael Abt to the crime scene to pick up some clothing and essentials on the Monday after the murders, he held an impromptu press conference on his front lawn. It was also a photo op. Michael was a popular subject for news photographers with his graphic T-shirts, faded denim jacket, and longish blond hair occasionally wrapped with a red paisley bandana.

He took questions from a huddle of reporters on his front lawn. Years later, he told me that a question I asked that day made the hair on the back of his neck stand up. It was: "What are you going to do, Michael. You're all alone now."

It sounds rude. I don't remember asking it, but it was 48 years ago, so maybe I did. Michael said it shook him because he had heard it before—in 1963.

He was a 10-year-old playing alone on the front lawn on Easter Sunday while his parents unpacked from the family's move into their new home. He said he heard a very distinct voice ask, "What are you going to do, Michael? You're all alone now."

He never forgot it. When I stood in roughly the same place and asked exactly the same question after his family had been murdered, it rattled him, but he didn't tell me for decades.

I still had a lot to learn about reporting in 1976, but I felt comfortable interviewing the Abts and their friends after the murders. Despite everything swirling around him, Clifford was a natural comedian. Michael was always polite and welcoming. We were all in the same general age bracket. Their parents' house, with the prayer over the thermostat and the standard, uncluttered, Irish American décor, could have been my parents'.

Like them, I came from a blue-collar family, part Irish American, and, like them, I was educated in Catholic and public schools. We grew up in different states, but we all played outside rather than in one of the basement recreation rooms popular in the '60s.

Like them, I lived near a dense wood and deep water. As kids, we all did things that might be considered ill-advised today. I sneaked into pools after hours, swung from vines over shallow creeks and jumped off a tall tower into an abandoned water-filled quarry. Their friends dropped fish tanks and storm windows off a quarry wall to hear the glass break. When televisions still had vacuum tubes, they'd throw old sets off and watch them implode.

In the autumn, they soaped up cardboard refrigerator boxes to use as sleds. They raced down steep hills of wild grasses, smushing the stalks with abandon as they went. They got bigger and bigger boxes to accommodate more kids.

In the winter, they made monster sleds out of car hoods from the salvage yard that hemmed the neighborhood. The owner's son brought hoods from early '60s junkers. They'd knock the hood ornaments off, wax the hoods, flip them over and jump inside. Five or six kids would barrel downhill, mowing saplings down as they zipped along. Once, they hit a full-size tree and all came flying off. It's a wonder nobody was killed, several of them said.

Decades later, business owner Ed Allahand discovered a rusted car hood on the hill. "It brought back such great memories," he said.

★★★

When the Abts and their friends were still in elementary school, they began playing in "the guy's yard." They'd hang out on the porch of a vacation bungalow owned by a man who only used it on occasional weekends. Because nobody knew his name, they referred to the property as "the guy's yard," as in, "I'll meet you at the guy's yard." They suspected the owner knew they were sitting on his porch and playing on his lawn, but they never crossed paths with him because, whenever his car was spotted, someone would shout that "the guy" was coming, and the kids would scatter into the woods or caves that ringed the neighborhood. As they grew, the same tribe of boys used the guy's lawn for hide-and-go-seek and then football. By 17, they were drinking beer on the guy's porch. As they entered adulthood, someone said, "Well, what the hell is the guy's name?"

***

With so many kids in the neighborhood, fights broke out, and, occasionally, one would feature an impromptu weapon like a tree branch and, once, a bow and arrow. One dustup at the guy's house was memorable because it involved strategic use of briar bushes.

Clifford, always one of the tallest boys, was trounced by a much smaller teen after he made the mistake of removing his jacket to fight while standing directly in front of the guy's sticker bushes. Ready to duke it out, Clifford reached his arms behind his back to pull his coat off. While his hands were still pinned behind his back, the jacket cuffs acting like handcuffs, the smaller kid leaned in. He shoved Clifford backwards into the thorny branches and jumped him. The sharp stickers made it impossible for him to roll away and escape. The smaller kid pummeled him.

***

Police continued to guard the murder scene at night to keep the evidence secure and to thwart cameramen. National magazines like *Official Detective* and *True Detective* were clamoring for crime scene photos.

After a few nights in the house, the guard detail moved to cars parked in the Abts' driveway. One cold evening, two officers were watching the house from a patrol car when Patrolman Dave Clee, who lived down the street, walked by. The three policemen started crabbing about higher-ups by name, never noticing that one of the officers inside the car was sitting on the open microphone.

Dispatcher Bill Fox heard it all, along with anyone who owned a police radio: "I was working the midnight shift and I heard somebody hit the mike," Fox said, laughing. "They were sitting in front of the house, watching it to preserve the evidence, and one of them hit the button on the mike so everyone could hear them talking about how scary it was to sit there. They were mad at the chief. They were saying, 'That fucking Larry Michaels. He's got us out here freezing while he's home in bed.' One said the killer, who was still on the loose, could be right behind them watching them for all they knew."

The officers had been broadcasting for several minutes when a patrol car from neighboring Lower Southampton Township came zipping up the street. The driver shouted, "Your mike's on."

***

The two multiple murders were the biggest news in the Philadelphia region, and reporters didn't want to miss any news updates. Some out-of-town newsmen replaced their regular meals with orange peanut butter crackers dropped from vending machines. I lived close enough to stop at my cabin for meals, but I had to buy new underwear at Neshaminy Mall because I didn't have time to lug my dirty clothes up the cliff and drive to a laundromat.

***

The murders had a ripple effect in Bensalem, even for children. A middle-school student told police that the Cornwells Heights boy who didn't show up to fight Johnny after school on March 12 felt very bad since he learned of Johnny's death. Karen Thorpe, the girl from the school bus who told Kathy she'd see her Monday, was brushing her teeth Saturday morning when she overheard a newscast about Kathy's murder. When Maria D'Ambrosio got off the school bus on Monday, a patrol car was waiting to follow her home. Police wanted to be certain the killer wasn't gunning for the papergirl, perhaps mistakenly thinking the 13-year-old had caught a glimpse of him.

Daily routine was totally upended for Michael and Clifford Abt. Their home was roped off as a crime scene for five days. And, because their family's killer or killers were still at large, police were concerned for their safety.

Detectives didn't publicize it, but they called in a psychologist to hypnotize Michael, hoping he might recall something that his conscious mind had erased. After he went under, he was able to recall which items he touched or moved when he entered the house but not much else.

★★★

For Bensalem detectives, the middle of March was go and go and go and then grab a couple of hours of sleep at nighttime when no one was available to be interviewed. Every day was overfilled. One detective said they interviewed everyone who knew an Abt—from Margie's boss to a man known by the street name Tennessee.

One of the most poignant interviews was with Peggy's coworker Kathleen Burman. Speaking through tears, Burman said that, in all the time Peggy had worked at the IRS, she had never heard her speak badly of anyone.

Ken McDowell, who worked with Jack at Bell Telephone for 20 years, told them the phone installer was a talkative guy with a good sense of humor. McDowell was impressed that Jack had built his own house.

Jim Carberry told police that Jack Abt often wore a jacket with a scout emblem.

Mike Scheswohl of 3744 Hollywood Avenue told the patrolman who came to his door that he didn't know if he had seen any of the Abts on March 12. He explained he had never met any of the Abts, and, since he didn't know them, he would not know if he saw one of them or not.

Ed Cooney drove by the Abt house about 5 p.m., but he didn't see anything amiss.

Nor did Bill Mayrer of 3715 Fleetwood.

Or Susan Rosenburger of 4803 Dara Faith Drive.

George Geschwendt had the best view of the Abt house from his home across the street. He was out of work, so he was home alone all day on March 12. He said he didn't see or hear anything out of the ordinary, though. He mentioned that he went to high school with Clifford.

Felix Iostracco said his dog never fails to bark and carry on whenever strangers come to the neighborhood, but the dog didn't bark at all that day.

★★★

If the Abt case were a detective novel, red herrings would have been planted in every chapter.

One boy who got off the school bus at Johnny's stop told police he followed Johnny through the kitchen door on March 12. He mentioned that the Abts' dog usually came running right to them when they walked into the kitchen, but he didn't see or hear the dog at all that day. The kid said he saw some glass near the threshold, but he said he wasn't sure if Johnny saw it. "He didn't say nothing about it," he said. "I noticed the glass on the outside. There was a little on the steps. I brushed it off with my foot."

The kid told police he stood by the door while Johnny, with his coat still on, took a bun off the kitchen countertop, stuck it in the oven and turned the oven on. They talked about a CB radio Johnny was going to get. The kid invited Johnny to his house. Johnny said he'd come over later. He wanted to check whether a neighbor was able to get a radiator for his Buick first.

The boy told police he left Johnny alone in the house and walked home. "He said he would try to be at my house by 4," the kid said, "but he never came."

Police interviewed him a second time on March 23. This time, the kid's mother told the detectives her son had some changes he wanted to make to his statement. He never actually went into the house. He just made the whole thing up.

Police were still interested, because the boy was outside the house minutes before Johnny was shot. A detective asked him if he heard a sound like a firecracker after Johnny walked into the house. He did not.

Police from one New Jersey town phoned to report that a man there confessed to killing the Abts. One glitch: He said the Abt family he killed definitely did not own a dog. The man later signed himself in to Ancora Psychiatric Hospital in Hammonton, New Jersey.

One woman phoned to report she once worked at a law firm where they had a lawyer named Apt, spelled with a "p" instead of a "b." She said several female employees there had made unsolicited amorous advances toward her. She thought maybe there was a connection between Abt and Apt.

A spooked 19-year-old insisted the Abts were killed by a man she met in Fairless Hills, a development about 10 miles from Trevose. She said the man sang weird chants and broke a baby's toys, and he told her he was a follower of Charlie Manson.

A woman who never met any of the Abts was baffled when detectives showed up at her apartment door asking questions about the slayings. She told them she had no idea what would make the police come to her apartment. After detectives learned she was mired in a lawsuit with her estranged husband and her father-in-law, they left, guessing one of them called the police to prank her.

Detectives interviewed the manager of the apartment building that was home to an Abt cousin who crowed that he knew who committed the murders. The apartment manager told the detectives her tenant had specifically instructed her to not to tell anyone anything about him, and he had stressed that meant people with badges too. Nevertheless, the woman instantly unspooled everything she knew about him. He moved in one month earlier. His rent was $170 a month. He didn't have a roommate. He worked as a draftsman. He owned a 1965 Ford. She gave them his license plate number and the name of his closest relative. She also told them he seemed like the quiet type.

★★★

To find the killer or killers, detectives had to ask intimate questions about the victims. Questions about Margie were largely unproductive. One young man was asked, "Did Margie get around pretty much?" He answered that he had only seen her with Gary. The follow-up question was, "Did she seem like she knew a lot of guys?" The answer to that one was, "No. She was a pretty quiet girl." When the questioning switched to Clifford, detectives got an unexpected earful.

When they asked a Philadelphia woman if Clifford had ever ripped anyone off, she said, "Yes, everybody." One man told detectives that he had shot up drugs in Clifford's bedroom. A neighbor suspected Clifford had stolen her engagement ring. One man said he saw Clifford driving a Monte Carlo with a loaded .357 magnum cocked on his lap.

One told police Clifford invited a drug dealer named Bug Eyes to live with his family for a month. A friend of Margie's told detectives she saw Clifford and his friends shooting up in the living room. One of Michael's friends said Clifford always had drugs in his room, but his parents refused to acknowledge it.

Several people insisted the killer was a North Carolina man who Clifford had burned in a $20,000 drug deal. A woman on the outs with Clifford griped that Jack and Peggy always covered up for him. She said "Stein" owed her $100 from a drug deal, but, whenever she called the Abt house, his parents would say he no longer lived there.

Several said Clifford was tied up with a shady character called "Teddy the Greek," who worked out of a diner on U.S. Route 1. As the investigation unfurled, others would come to the intake window at the township police station to dish on Clifford.

My very limited experience with Clifford was different. One night, when I went into the house to ask if the police had shared any news, I absentmindedly parked my newish dark-brown Toyota Corolla opposite the Abts' driveway around sunset. An hour later, Clifford and his fiancée, Shelly, approached me in the living room. Clifford said he didn't see my car in the dark, and he backed into it. There was no damage to his father's much bigger station wagon, he said, but my rear fender was crumpled.

We went out to inspect the damage. He offered to pay for the repair. I thought for a half-second, then said, "Don't worry about it." On a suburban reporter's salary, I didn't have the money to repair it right away, but I knew I couldn't hand car-repair estimates to someone who had attended his family's mass funeral two days earlier. While Shelly and I stood by shivering, Clifford yanked the fender away so the car was drivable.

Clifford didn't have to tell me he hit my car. With the number of cars moving in and out of the driveway that dark winter night, I would have had no idea who hit it.

***

In 1976, police had no dashboard computers, and cellphones were still 20 years off. Reporters and crime buffs could buy inexpensive police scanners to monitor police radios, so any detective who turned up information he didn't want to share over the airwaves had to drive to a public phone booth and put a dime in the coin slot to get three minutes of talk time. Detectives kept rolls of dimes in their glove compartments.

***

Just to track down the shoe that left its bloody print in the Abts' basement before the advent of shoeprint databases, police had to phone shoe manufacturers one by one. They narrowed it down to an oil-resistant, lifetime-guaranteed, non-marking sole manufactured by the Quabaug Rubber Company. They must have felt lucky to catch shift foreman Ken Fairbrother on the phone at Quahoag's Massachusetts factory. He was the last person left in the building the day they called. Most Quabaug workers had already rushed home in advance of a heavy March snowstorm. The detectives' initial elation probably faded when Fairbrother let them know Quabaug only made the soles. They shipped them to shoe manufacturers nationwide.

Detective Eckert checked the soles of every shoe on display at one Neshaminy Mall store. He didn't want to let it slip why he was there, so he told the salesperson he needed a particular sole. His effort paid off. The $32.99 boot that left its bloody impression in the basement came from the shoe department at Sears, just two miles from the murder scene.

***

A few days after the slayings, it became clear that the glitches several people in the Abts' orbit faced on March 12 were actually blessings in disguise. Clifford's jail sentence was a stroke of luck for him because he was safely behind bars on March 12. Shelly Robbins, the single mother he was engaged to, missed dinner at the Abts because she was too bushed to drive to Trevose. That meant she also missed becoming the killer's seventh victim. Michael missed his fish dinner, but he also missed the killer. The Abts' third son Johnny wasn't so lucky.

***

Lucky wasn't quite the right word for the Abts who survived by happenstance. Fewer than 24 hours after Michael's family was slaughtered, a photographer popped up from behind a bush and shouted for him to give him a big smile. The 21-year-old, his cheeks crimson from tears, was floored. When a different photographer raised his camera outside the police station to snap a picture later that day, Michael lurched toward him. He didn't want his photo published while the killer or killers were still at large. The medication his doctor prescribed couldn't calm his fears that the gunmen might be coming after him, too. When Chief Michaels put an arm around Michael to comfort him in the police station parking lot, a cameraman with a long lens captured a shot of them from the back. It appeared in the next day's paper.

***

Clifford's fiancée's mother told reporters the 23-year-old was so heartsick over losing his family that he might have a nervous breakdown if he couldn't get out of jail. She hired a former state senator as his attorney.

She lent Clifford $669 to pay his court costs—about $3,500 in today's dollars. He never would have been jailed if he had simply paid his fine when he was arrested on a forgery charge two years earlier. A sympathetic judge had given him pretrial probation, so he would have had no criminal record if he just paid his fines. When a random check revealed he didn't, he was jailed on contempt of court charges the Monday before the murders.

Authorities assumed Clifford was safe in Bucks County Prison, but his new attorney Rob Rovner had misgivings. He told police a hired killer who did not know the individual family members might have thought he murdered a sixth Abt when he shot similarly built Gary Engle. If the killer were a newspaper reader, he would realize he got the wrong man.

Chief Michaels, taking no chances, moved Clifford to the holding cell at his own well-staffed station for safekeeping. The Abts' oldest was at least six feet tall, but he bunked on a narrow, 66-inch-long metal frame in the holding cell at the station. There was no mattress. Clifford never complained. He told me he was glad to be back in Bensalem and grateful the police officers protected him and treated him well. They brought him pizza and McDonald's.

While he was in the police station, Clifford overheard the people lined up in the lobby to badmouth him. Like a swimmer caught in an undertow, he was overwhelmed. He had lost his parents, his youngest brother, his two sisters, and now neighbors and casual acquaintances were serving up unsavory details about him. There were plenty.

Acquaintances made it sound as if Clifford should have a warning label plastered on his back. A woman said Clifford's car blew up. Neighbors reported cars with out-of-state license plates making quick, unexplained stops at the intersection of Fleetwood Avenue and Dara Faith Drive. One said there's just too much traffic up Dara Faith for a road that goes practically nowhere.

One said drug traffic in the area had slowed since Clifford's arrest. He emphasized Clifford was the only person at the Abt house who was linked to criminal activity: "Not the Abts—an Abt," he said. "Clifford. That's all."

The idea that an elusive madman shot six people in their neighborhood was so staggering to Trevose residents that some breathed easier when they heard police were focusing on drug connections. They could morally exclude the casualties of a drug war, viewing themselves as a cut above all that, and feel safer in that knowledge.

Clifford said he knew the detectives were looking at him and wondering, "Who hated you so much they'd take out your family?" He had lain awake at night in Bucks County Prison turning that over in his head. It bedeviled him. He couldn't think of a single person so unglued that they would have killed his mother and his little brother and sister for revenge.

***

Police tracked several leads—a drug deal gone wrong, a vendetta against the family, perhaps a motorcycle gang grudge because Clifford's fiancée was a biker's ex-wife.

On Tuesday, four days after the murders, police were still referring to "the killer or killers."

A patrol lieutenant said whoever did it didn't go into the house to burglarize or rob; they went in to kill.

As the investigation entered its fifth day, District Attorney Ken Biehn said police were interviewing "anybody who walks."

Chief Michaels said it could be a "professional hit" or a "local nut." He was getting warmer.

One officer joked, "One of these days we're going to find somebody standing stark naked at Gino's preaching the gospel, and that will be our boy."

***

Officer Clee checked the interior of the Abt house nightly while it was still a crime scene. Usually, he had Blackjack, his pet Doberman, at his side. Blackjack would enter the house, but he'd stall when his nostrils connected with something near the swinging doors to the basement. As Clee put it, "Blackjack always put his brakes on when he got to the steps."

★★★

One day while the house was still a crime scene, Chief Michaels held court for a handful of reporters at the front door. Without being asked, he offered up that the Abts' living room rug was full of dog hair. He added that his own wife never would have kept house that way.

★★★

On Tuesday, March 16, Chief Michaels told reporters he was trying to bring Michael down from alcohol and prescription tranquilizers so that he could attend his family's funeral the next day. "Michael is six feet off the ground," he announced. A reporter who watched Michael crying and clinging to friends at the police station described him in print as a tightly coiled spring ready to explode.

Michael and his extended family faced a task that day that few families ever must—finding 30 pallbearers for the funeral Mass the next day at Saint Dominic Roman Catholic Church in Northeast Philadelphia.

Chief Michaels ordered police protection for Michael and Clifford at the Mass. He told reporters there was a possibility the murderer or murderers still wanted them dead.

CHAPTER 8

An Unforgettably Somber Saint Patrick's Day

> "We have no new leads," he said. "All I can say now is that even my mother is still a suspect."
>
> —POLICE CHIEF LARRY MICHAELS

Twenty-five years after Peggy Abt walked down the aisle at Saint Dominic Roman Catholic Church on her wedding day, her casket was wheeled up the same wide aisle, along with her husband Jack's, their son Johnny's, and their daughters Margie's and Kathy's.

This time, twelve police officers directed traffic outside the church. Plainclothes detectives mingled with the worshippers. A patrolman filmed the crowd, hoping Peggy's killer might show up for her funeral.

Twelve of the Abts' pallbearers arrived at the church in a school bus—Kathy's and Johnny's middle school classmates. As the church was filling up for the 10 a.m. Mass, the children were taught how to glide their friends' coffins to the front of the church on wheeled trolleys called biers.

Some of Michael and Clifford's friends who could not afford proper funeral attire waited in the cold vestibule at the front of the church to offer their condolences.

Inside the church, hundreds of sniffling mourners turned in their pews to watch a dozen solemn pallbearers heading up the wide center aisle with the black caskets that held the bodies of Jack, 49, and Peggy, 48.

They were quickly followed by six more pallbearers with the silver-gray casket with 19-year-old Margie's body inside.

Moans came from the pews as 16 teary-eyed children from Neil Armstrong Middle School guided the caskets of Kathy, 12, and Johnny, 13, up the aisle. Even decades later, Michael recalled how that sight crushed him. "The worst thing I ever saw was their classmates carrying them. Those poor little kids carrying their friends to their graves," he said.

Only four of the five caskets were covered by white palls, the traditional linens used in Catholic funerals to signify a shared belief in eternal life. The church ran out.

A chorus of sobs rose from the crowd when Clara Abt, Jack's 84-year-old mother, slowly made her way down the aisle past the five coffins, with relatives helping her.

Then, mourners gasped as 75-year-old Margaret Haney, Peggy's mother, appeared with her lips quivering, looking as if she would collapse if not supported by others.

More muffled sobs came from across the church when the two surviving sons walked up the aisle with young women on their arms. Their tremendous loss was palpable and irreparable.

Michael took a seat surrounded by about 20 family members. A detective guided Clifford, his fiancée and his lawyer to a seat near the wall. He was still in police custody.

Gary Mitchell, the 12-year-old who was going to meet Johnny to go fishing Saturday morning, arrived late for Mass. He had never been to a funeral before. Seeing five coffins in a row stunned him.

Fifteen-year-old Bill Haney, an Abt cousin, could not believe his eyes when he saw five caskets. He remembers people staring sadly as he and his family members took their places at the front of the church.

Rev. Richard Farrant, the cousin of Peggy Abt who married the couple, would bury them.

His voice cracked when he asked mourners not to allow bitterness to enter their hearts against the person or persons responsible for "our Friday night massacre."

Five other clergymen took part in the funeral service, including the Rev. Lawrence Abt, Jack Abt's brother. Jack had converted to Catholicism when he married Peggy, but his brother helmed a Baptist church in New Jersey.

Clifford spent most of the nearly one-hour Mass staring at the side wall of the church and clenching his fiancée's hand so tightly that his fingers were flushed pink. He never looked toward the long center aisle, which was more than half-filled with his loved ones' caskets.

Michael sat in the center aisle and glanced at the caskets often. He wept on and off throughout the Mass, and he left the church briefly during Holy Communion.

Clifford knew he was being watched, and he maneuvered to get out of the spotlight. Michael knew he was being watched and seemed more at home with the cameras.

When the priest waved burning incense over the caskets to symbolize the five souls' ascension into heaven, a sharp burst of uncontrolled tears issued from the people in the pews. Eighth-grader Carolyn Hiteshew bolted from a pew near the front of the church and ran outside sobbing. She told a reporter she was Kathy's best friend.

The service took just short of an hour. Afterwards, Michael was led away from his pew in tears. Clifford and his fiancée quietly left the church.

A light gray cloud of incense stalled over the center aisle as more than 300 mourners exited into the fresh, frigid air outside. The funeral bells tolled overhead as about three-quarters of the mourners turned to walk toward the sprawling cemetery behind the church.

As they walked the length of the imposing brownstone church, they were probably unaware it was designed by a Confederate soldier who fought at Gettysburg. After the war, Henry Roby put out an architect's shingle. In 1896, he designed Saint Dominic's with pointed arches, a ribbed vault ceiling, narrow lancet windows and other Victorian Gothic flourishes.

As black skies threatened overhead, undertakers scrambled to load the coffins into five black hearses lined up in front of the church. Because funeral directors rarely need five hearses, John F. Fluehr & Sons rented four of them from a livery service.

Snow flurries were falling from the sky by the time the first shivering mourners reached the burial site behind the church. A knot of older women stood inches from the open graves, some in the pillbox-style hats that Jackie Kennedy made popular in the early '60s and a few in old-fashioned black lace mantillas that covered their heads and reached for their shoulders.

Michael had donned a thick, pile-lined jacket over his funeral attire for the unpleasantly cold walk to the cemetery. Clifford wore a thin, dark suit with no overcoat despite the gusty wind.

Two gravesites had been readied. Jack and Peggy Abt would be buried on top of each other. Three of their children would be buried alongside them, their coffins stacked. Peggy Abt's mother Margaret Haney owned the cemetery plot. She had buried her husband Bill there two years earlier, and, in 11 more years, she would join him.

The crowd turned as one and watched in silence when the first hearse climbed over the horizon and clambered down the narrow cemetery road toward them.

Then the second hearse rose over the horizon. Then another and another and another. It was a dismal sight.

The monstrous loss sunk in as hundreds of eyes darted from hearse to hearse. One newspaper columnist wrote, "You had to count them. You couldn't help it."

The drivers slowly realized there were too many hearses to park near the gravesite. After some jockeying, they formed a long black line that extended out the cemetery gates. The last four drivers waited patiently while John Abt's coffin was lifted from the first hearse.

About 40 yards away, a conventional burial was proceeding under a canopy. A single coffin was removed from a single hearse. Mourners there must have been surprised when the fifth hearse pulled up to the Abt-Haney plot.

As the last of the caskets was unloaded, the knot of mourners tightened around the open graves. As the priest began the prayers committing his family to the earth, Clifford stood at the outside edge of the large circle, his upper teeth biting his bottom lip, shivering from the cold. Flanked by his fiancée and his attorney, tears welled up in his eyes as he listened to the priest's words from a distance.

Michael stood front and center, inches from the five caskets and surrounded by aunts and uncles and grandmothers and photographers. Cameras clicked as he bent from the waist to kiss each coffin before it was lowered into the ground. Two friends supported him as he left the gravesite.

Clifford convulsed in tears only once, when one of his grandmothers approached him as she was leaving and scolded him: "Please make a man of yourself, for my sake." She likely didn't realize how much the murders had affected him. His lightweight suit covered the week-old prison tattoo with the badly drawn heart and the words "Mom" and "Dad." It was a defining moment for Clifford, and one he wouldn't forget.

As mourners left the cemetery, Michael approached the ones he recognized and said, "Thank you for coming. Thank you for coming."

Before the children from Neil Armstrong Middle School left for their waiting school bus, they placed green and white carnations on their friends' caskets, marking a cheerless Saint Patrick's Day. Most of the boys were red-eyed as they turned to leave for their school bus. As the girls headed out, they sobbed openly and wrapped their arms around one another.

Some parents opted not to let their children attend the Mass because the killer or killers were still at large and they feared gunplay might break out at the church.

Mourners left the cemetery road clasping holy cards that read, "In Loving Memory of John F. Abt Sr., Margaret A. Abt, Margaret M. Abt, John F. Abt Jr., Kathleen Abt. Died March 12, 1976."

After the service, Clifford returned to the holding cell in the Bensalem Police Department.

Two rectangular granite stones were ordered to mark the Abt graves at Saint Dominic's, one for John F. Sr. and Margaret A., and one for their children: John F. Jr, Margaret M. and Kathleen. The engravers would add their birth years—1927, 1928, 1956, 1962 and 1963. The year of death was the same for all five: 1976.

Michael completed an application to the Veterans Administration to get a flat bronze marker and a small flag holder added to the gravesite to honor his father as a World War II veteran.

After the funeral, Father Farrant told a reporter that he saw Jack and Peggy several times each year since their wedding 27 years earlier, and they seemed to have grown fonder of one another and more appreciative of their marriage.

He also mentioned that he had heard about the slayings on the radio the day after they happened, but he originally thought it must be a different Abt family.

As the stragglers walked to their cars, Chief Michaels told a *Philadelphia Inquirer* reporter that he had hoped his men might produce a suspect at the funeral, but they had failed to do so. "We have no new leads," he said. "All I can say now is that even my mother is still a suspect."

While the chief kibbitzed with reporters, Lieutenant Zajac stayed on the case and away from cameras and microphones. He was busy following a hunch. Before the next week was out, he and his detectives would crack the case.

★★★

After the funeral, some of the Abts' old friends headed to the Scottsville Inn for lunch. Just 11 days earlier, they had gathered there to sing "Happy Birthday" to Jack Abt. The mood at the lunch was heavy, but it would pick up again that evening for the inn's Saint Patrick's Day celebration.

★★★

The family of Gary Engle, the killer's sixth victim, was busy arranging a private burial in suburban Sunset Memorial Park four miles from the crime scene. They had learned of their nephew's death by chance via a radio news report the previous Saturday. Gary was buried with the grandparents who raised him. Their shared cemetery marker was inscribed with the words, "Together Forever."

★★★

The next day, Edward and Marguerite Vogenberger were interred at the Middletown Friends Meeting Cemetery, a 1700s Quaker burial ground a short walk from their home.

It was still unclear what, if anything, their killers took, but a police search of the farmhouse turned up a bag filled with hundreds of dollars' worth of quarters, dimes and nickels they'd left behind.

CHAPTER 9

Covering a Spree Murder

Ed Allahand remembered a night when the lyrics to Queen's five-month-old hit "Bohemian Rhapsody" were playing in the living room at the Abt house. The soundtrack eerily fit what happened inside the house on March 12. As they listened, it dawned on each person that the lyrics were a mashup of what had occurred right where they were sitting.

With the killer or killers still at large a week after the killings, the Abt brothers were angry, on edge and afraid the killer might still be hunting them.

Clifford stayed at the family house on and off after he was released from jail, but he and Michael had to be physically separated once. Word had gotten back to Clifford that Michael was checking up on his acquaintances to see if any of them killed the family. Stunned and humiliated, Clifford said, "I think I was hurt by that as much as I was by the news of this thing happening."

Clifford, with a theatrical shrug, told me he had not completely ruled Michael out as a suspect. Although Clifford rarely made eye contact, it was clear he said it just to shock. He didn't really think his younger brother was responsible for the horror in the basement. As one of the police officers said later, "Clifford was a wiseass."

One day, Clifford told me the killer probably didn't know much about guns because he fired at a funny angle. Usually aloof and even distant, when he spoke about the shootings, his fingers tightened into half fists. As his eyes ricocheted around the bullet-scarred rooms where it happened, his usual, deep voice turned higher and halting.

Michael and Clifford could neither relax nor grieve as long as the killer was free. Detectives, working day and night, had good reason to like one local man for it, but he sat for a polygraph and passed it.

"Murder is usually the easiest crime to solve," Chief Michaels said. "Most of the time, you have a motive, and most of the time, the doer is easy to find because he has some clear connection with the person killed. We just haven't found that here."

With no new leads from the police station, reporters turned to Michael and Clifford to keep the murder story alive. Cameramen trailed Michael, who seemed in perpetual motion. He was more available than his brooding older brother, and he was more likely to do something that would make a good picture. The best newspaper photos are candid shots that catch subjects doing something unexpected.

Michael, with his dad's never-met-a-stranger approach to others, became every reporter's default interview subject. His genial manner put skittish reporters at ease, and his quotable offhand remarks got every one of us scribbling in our notebooks. While the killer was still on the loose, he quipped, "I've been using a 12-gauge shotgun for a pillow every night." He wasn't kidding. He had borrowed one from a friend.

Clifford would talk to me for a story if we were both downstairs at the same time, but he generally headed straight upstairs to avoid reporters.

Journalists from at least eight daily papers vied for the latest details on the Abt and Vogenberger murders, trying to herd all the facts they could before their deadlines. If you missed your deadline, your facts would grow cold, because the next newspaper was 24 hours off.

Big city papers regularly sold a half-million copies a day in the years before CNN and online news. Even a small suburban paper could sell 65,000 copies a day. Reporters were expected to feed the beast with fresh news for every edition.

Writers who turned in what city editors called "good reads" could be hired away by bigger newspapers with bigger salaries and bigger circulation. Most reporters were more interested in bigger stories than bigger salaries. If money had been their goal, they wouldn't have gone into journalism.

That didn't mean they weren't competitive. One experienced reporter was so cutthroat that he was rumored to carry a roll of tape and an "out of order" sign in his briefcase so he could stick the sign on one of the pay phones near a big event to reserve it for his own use.

Lazy reporters buddied up to politicians or police chiefs, never writing anything unflattering so they'd get a scoop when a big story came around. Conscientious ones stuck to the facts, recognizing they worked at papers of record, and their stories might someday be used by historians. Newspapers are considered first-person sources for historians because reporters are on the scene at historic events interviewing witnesses.

If the story were big enough, it would attract some star reporter from a bigger city who wrote like he believed his words were performative. One Philadelphia television reporter arrived at the county courthouse in a helicopter and kept her sunglasses on inside as we awaited the jury verdict.

Most of us on my 60,000-circulation suburban daily were still learning the business, and we tried different styles of newswriting. One reporter wrote this about Michael's friendliness: "Michael's hospitality toward the press, however, may be motivated by a more profound need than simply attention. One senses that Michael fears being alone because then he will have to deal head on with his family's tragedy. Thus, he is trying to insulate himself ..."

One awkward observation about Michael's physique made it into print: "His strong facial features are those of the classic, all-American Nordic ideal. He has an athletic physique with a tapered waist that flares into broad shoulders from which hang well-defined, muscular arms."

After that was published, it's no wonder Michael studied the television screen when he spotted himself on the evening news. With cameras constantly clicking feet from his face, he became an instant celebrity. He didn't seek publicity, but, after several days of coverage, he would pull his longish hair behind his ears and straighten up to his full height when the cameramen came closer.

A quick study, Michael picked up newspaper jargon in days. He crabbed that the city papers weren't giving enough press to his friend,

Gary Engle. "You'd never know Gary Engle was killed too," he said. "I'm really sorry to see he's not getting the same coverage."

Most reporters didn't understand how Michael's and Clifford's lives were suddenly and irreparably shuffled by the slaughter. I know I didn't. It didn't hit me until decades later that I first met them during the worst week of their lives.

Michael was actually waking up with cold sweats, roused by dreams that the killer was bursting out at him from behind the living room wall, sudden terror on a loop, like a sordid sequel to the movie *Groundhog Day*. He was so jumpy that he had to stare at a television screen halfway into the night before he could relax enough to nod off to nightmares.

With prescriptions and whiskey, he navigated his new normal, a spot where few people have ever been. It started when that photographer popped out of a bush and asked for a big smile. It went on for decades.

Gawkers stopped their cars in front of the house, and, if Michael or Clifford happened to be walking to the mailbox, husbands pointed them out to their wives. "People must have some kind of weird disease the way whole families stop their cars and stare at my house," Michael said at the time.

Academic studies that didn't exist in 1976 now say people who lose a family member to a violent death often are more stressed than people who survive violent crimes themselves. The research shows members of "homicide families," as sociologists dub them, sometimes change their beliefs about themselves and others. Some feel numb. Some feel intense grief. Some feel stigmatized. Many fear for their own safety.

They may feel guilty or responsible for the killings. Often, their relationships with family members are strained. They may even suspect relatives are involved in the homicide. Sometimes they are preoccupied with revenge. Their dreams often replay images of the violent death. They may become anxious on the victims' birthdays and favorite holidays and whenever they face reminders of the event. They have to face police, reporters, prosecutors and defense attorneys. All those stressors sometimes lead to divorce, drug use and alcohol abuse.

The homicide families in the studies lost a single family member. Michael and Clifford lost their parents, their sisters, their younger brother and a close friend on the same day.

And, at first, they believed the family annihilator might still be gunning for them, too. As Michael put it, "Whoever did it didn't finish the job."

★★★

Police officers and others involved in the investigation dealt with their feelings privately in the '70s. The mandated psychologist sessions as seen on *Law & Order* weren't a thing yet. That was true for ambulance crews and firefighters and reporters on the periphery of the investigation, too.

"You kind of kept your emotions out of it while you were working," Detective Eckert said. "Getting what I needed to get the job done came first. You really become hardened to it. It was just part of the job."

Carolyn Per, a writer who lived five miles from the Abts, captured the mood in Trevose when she said, "It just felt so incredible."

★★★

The March 19 announcement that the fairy-tale marriage of Britain's Princess Margaret was coming apart was the lead story in the next edition of the *New York Times*, but it didn't even make the front page of the next *Courier Times*. The *Courier* reserved its front-page for the Abts and the Vogenbergers, the biggest news in suburban Philadelphia that week.

Some readers were aghast when they learned Michael had moved back into his parents' house after police released it. It made sense to me. Our reactions are based on the information we know. If all you know is that a killer crouched by the piano and committed six horrific murders, moving back seems eerie. Michael and Clifford knew more, though. They could go back in time in their minds and recall their mother playing that piano. They could recall barbecues and birthday parties and Christmas mornings at the house their father built.

Despite grim reminders as small as the chip shot out of the upstairs toilet and as large as the basement stairs removed as evidence, Michael felt he couldn't just pack up and leave his home. His nightmares travelled with him, anyway. "If I go to the mountains, I'm still going to have flashbacks to that day," he said. "That's something I have to cope with no matter where I live."

If decision trees existed in the '70s—those charts that look like tree branches going in different directions based on the answers you give—Michael's and Clifford's trees wouldn't have many branches, at least until their parents' estates were settled.

Clifford was unemployed. Michael was laid off for winter. One day, Michael opened his wallet to show a reporter $48, and then he rooted in his jeans pockets to unearth another 45 cents. He told him it was all the money he had in the world.

Crime-scene cleanup companies were still 20 years off in the '70s. The sad task of scrubbing blood and spackling bullet holes usually fell to family members, but the police department dispatched Officer Clee to mitigate the blood in the Abt house before they released the house to Michael and Clifford.

Clee's mop swabbed the surface blood in the basement, but concrete is porous, and, with seven large blood pools, some soaked in. Michael's friends spent almost four hours on their hands and knees, scouring the floor with detergent and disinfectants. A cardboard box stationed by the basement door quickly filled with fetid rags. Joan Tomlinson, 21, was taken aback when she applied water to a brown stain and watched it turn crimson again, as if the bodies had just been lifted away.

One day Michael was a fun-loving 21-year-old who lived at home in a busy, loving family of seven. Two weeks later, he was mostly alone in his parents' four-bedroom house with bloodstains in the basement, bullet holes in the kitchen and a good-sized rectangle of missing carpet in the living room where his little brother, Johnny, fell. His family was in tatters. He said he was lonelier than he'd ever been. "I had to grow up overnight," he said. "I miss my family so damn much."

The Abts celebrated birthdays in January, March, April, May, July and twice in August. Suddenly, those birthdays were just sad reminders. In 1975, Michael had marked his milestone 21st birthday at a barbecue in his family's yard and an impromptu party at the Scottsville Inn. Two months after the murders, he marked his 22nd with a melancholy road trip to sparsely populated Sullivan County where Gary Engle grew up.

Wherever he went, Michael missed his father, whom he called his best friend, and his mother, who was game to attend an occasional rock concert with him even though the well-coiffed 48-year-old mother of five looked like one of the images that don't belong from an elementary school workbook when she took her seat in the drug-fueled crowd. "I don't care how bad I got, they always understood me," Michael said. "What happened to them stopped me dead in my tracks. I was destroyed. I couldn't feel love or hate. Just mad. It just killed me emotionally."

There was a sideshow atmosphere inside the house when the sons first got the place back. Drinks flowed. Stereo speakers competed with television news in the living room. Police and reporters and young men came and went.

It was the mid-'70s, so some visitors smoked, downed a Pabst or a Schaefer, or just listened to Peter Frampton's soft guitar work on his biggest hit to that point, "Show Me the Way." The lyrics about a man feeling he's going down and needing someone to show him the way fit the Abt brothers.

Michael's load-bearing friends, whose ages hovered around 22, did their best to help him manage a predicament few people ever face—being a survivor of a mass murder. The social center of the house shifted from the kitchen where the Abts were ambushed to a sunny corner of the living room where comfortable furniture was arranged around a heavy teak coffee table that Michael and his father had built.

Some friends brought beer and food. Some just hung out. One day a friend's toddler ran around the house carrying a toy machine gun. Michael's friends let him set the agenda.

After Michael's face flashed across televisions for a week, young women sought him out as if he were a rock star. One day a young woman with one of the short wedge haircuts that Olympic skater Dorothy Hamill made popular that year tried to attract his attention by showing off her mood ring in the living room. The trendy rings boasted thermal liquid crystals that change color based on the wearer's body temperature. The schtick was certain colors revealed the wearer's mood. Yellow showed nervousness. Pink showed contentment. Lavender indicated passion and romance. Brown revealed frustration. Orange revealed the wearer was feeling a little devilish. A black ring flagged the wearer as fearful or maybe just overworked. The woman with the wedge announced that her ring's blue color indicated she was calm and at ease.

Ed Allahand remembered a night when the lyrics to Queen's five-month-old hit "Bohemian Rhapsody" were playing in the living room at the Abt house. The soundtrack eerily fit what happened inside the kitchen and living room on March 12. As they listened, it dawned on each person that the lyrics were a mashup of what had occurred right where they were sitting. First, the acapella line that mirrored the stranger-than-fiction events that happened feet from their seats. The line about putting a gun against a man's head was a glove fit in a house where a killer lay in wait by the family piano. The exhortation to carry on as if nothing really matters seemed haunting as it rang out inside the house where six innocent people perished.

"We all just looked at each other," Allahand said. "We said this is a creepy song because that just happened here."

Others in Bensalem had the same reaction independently. Retired Patrolman Bill Fox said his thoughts go to the Abt killings whenever "Bohemian Rhapsody" comes on, even to this day.

Michael and Clifford had to carry on, as the song says, and do it without their parents' advice or financial support. In addition, their family's murder case was still a whodunnit.

CHAPTER 10

No Levittown

Suddenly, anyone who was an Abt or knew an Abt or had a sliver of new information about the investigation was sought after. At least two girls told reporters they were Kathy's best friend, and two boys anointed themselves Johnny's.

If Jack and Peggy Abt had a crystal ball when they picked a home site in Trevose in the early '60s, they likely never would have budged from their one-story brick twin on a manicured block in Northeast Philadelphia.

They weren't a couple who could simply fall smitten with a model house and write a check. For them, buying a house in the suburbs required sweat equity and moving twice. First, they sold their twin home and moved their growing family into an apartment near Northeast Philadelphia Airport. Then they used the money from the sale to buy a lot at the top of Dara Faith Drive and have a shell home erected there—a foundation, a frame, siding, a roof, doors and windows. Jack spent his nights and weekends installing electricity and plumbing, wallboard and flooring and cabinets and tile. Peggy always told the kids they did it on a wing and a prayer.

The two homes were only seven miles apart, but the Trevose neighborhood was as much an Adventureland for kids as Tom Sawyer's fictional Saint Petersburg, Missouri. Their new block was ringed by woods and farm fields and a massive salvage yard. The wider neighborhood boasted caves, cliffs, hiding places, trees to climb, a pond for ice-skating and a gem of a candy store inside a one-car garage. Massive granite slabs known as "The 84 Steps" led the way down to the wide brown Neshaminy Creek.

Kids milling in front of the Abt house the morning after the murders. Several sported Flyers gear. The city's NHL expansion team had won the Stanley Cup two years running. Neighbors were unaware the mass murderer was walking among them that morning. (From *The Philadelphia Inquirer* © 1976 Philadelphia Inquirer, LLC. All rights reserved. Used under license. Photographer Alexander Deans. Photograph provided courtesy of Special Collections Research Center, Temple University Libraries)

Kathryn Canavan as she looked on her 1977 press badge, a year after the murders and trial.

Dave Clee was a 29-year-old patrolman who had never seen a murder victim when he discovered six bodies in a neighbor's basement. When he called the police station to report it, the officer on the other end of the line thought he was pranking him. (Courtesy of Clee family)

Lieutenant Ted Zajac helmed the investigation. His wife Pat said he always knew when someone was lying, even in social situations. (Courtesy of Zajac family)

Peggy and Margie Abt visit the Scottsville Inn, the Trevose tavern where Jack Abt celebrated his 49th birthday six days before his death.

Johnny Abt (front center) and his sister Kathy (far right) celebrate a family birthday several years before the murders. (Courtesy of Dr. Bill Haney)

Kathy Abt was 12 years old when she was shot. A classmate said she was nice, not like some of the other popular girls. (Courtesy of Michael Abt and Special Collections Research Center, Temple University Libraries)

Margie and Jack Abt in a family photo. (Courtesy of Michael Abt and Special Collections Research Center, Temple University Libraries.)

Margie Abt liked to travel, and she had already reserved two summer weeks for her vacation. One was the week of July 12, the same week her killer's trial began.

Mourners' eyes followed the five black hearses as they proceeded down a hill toward the burial site on March 17. One news columnist wrote, "You had to count them." (Harry Sircely, Bucks County *Courier Times*, courtesy of Mary Ann Sircely)

Michael Abt bent to kiss each of the five coffins before they were lowered into the ground—his father's, his mother's, his two sisters' and his younger brother's. (From *The Philadelphia Inquirer* © 1976 Philadelphia Inquirer, LLC. All rights reserved. Used under license. Photographer Joseph McGuinn. Photograph provided courtesy of Special Collections Research Center, Temple University Libraries)

In Loving Memory of
JOHN F. ABT, SR.
MARGARET A. ABT
MARGARET M. ABT
JOHN F. ABT, JR.
KATHLEEN ABT
Died March 12, 1976

Let us Pray

Almighty God, through the death of Your Son on the cross, you have overcome death for us. Through his burial and resurrection from the dead you have made the grave a holy place and restored to us eternal life. We pray for those who died believing in Jesus and are buried with him in the hope of rising again. God of the living and the dead, may those who faithfully believed in you on earth praise you for ever in the joy of heaven. We ask this through Christ our Lord.

Amen.

Mourners left the funeral Mass with this holy card listing five members of the Abt family, all of whom died on March 12, 1976.

Peggy Abt's family members were buried with her parents. Margie's, Johnny's and Kathy's coffins were stacked on the left and Peggy and Jack were buried on the right. The gravestones of all five carry the same year of death—1976.

George Geschwendt was booked for six murders after he failed a polygraph and confessed. He told the polygraph operator he rarely let his emotions out, so shooting six people was somewhat of a relief for him. (Bensalem Township Police Department)

Rich Fink was known for his hard work and long hours defending clients no one else wanted, but he was also known as a practical joker who never lost his sense of humor despite the long odds predicted for some of his clients. (Courtesy of Richard R. Fink)

When George Geschwendt, Bill Fox and Clifford Abt shared a math class at Bensalem High, they sat in the same row. Geschwendt sat in the front, Fox in the middle and Abt in the back. Six years later they all played a part in the Abt slayings—Clifford Abt as a family member, Bill Fox as police, and George Geschwendt as the doer. (*The Owl*, the 1970 Bensalem High School Yearbook)

The Abt family in the early 1970s, taken from a larger photo of their extended family. Front row from left: Kathy, Johnny and Margie. Back row from left: Jack, Clifford, Michael and Peggy. (Abt family photo, courtesy of Dr. Bill Haney)

Backyards were studded with sheds and barbecue grills and above-ground pools. Driveways brimmed with cars, motorcycles and the occasional pickup converted to a camper. Do-it-yourselfers abounded. Neighbors helped each other with repairs. Painting got done when there was time and money. It was the '60s, so men did most of the heavy lifting. Most of them could take apart a car and put it together better.

If someone got sick, neighbors brought him food. If he were out of work, they tried to get him a job. Generally, if any man said a foul word in front of a woman, he apologized.

Like Jack Abt coldcocking the teenagers who trashed his lawn, Trevose residents often handled troublemakers without benefit of police. When a driver passing a knot of young men on a corner shouted a sexually tinged slur, one man from the corner raced to his own car, tailed the offender, forced his car off the road, jumped out and stomped on the man's car hood hard enough to dent it.

The Abts weren't the only family in the neighborhood to transform a shell. The Mitchell home at 3838 Fleetwood Avenue, completed in 1962, was so similar to the Abt place that police borrowed their blueprints to build courtroom exhibits.

★★★

The first thing I noticed the first time my car climbed Dara Faith Drive into the neighborhood was that Trevose was no Levittown. Levittown, the quintessential '50s American suburb, was just 11 miles away. Its 42 separate professionally planned neighborhoods were a postwar phenomenon.

Levitt & Sons, America's biggest home builders in the '50s, developed three Levittowns, one each in New York, New Jersey and Pennsylvania. They used assembly-line construction. Workers moved from lot to lot to pour slabs, frame houses, install electricity and plumbing and washing machines. Appliances, trees and shrubs were included.

Buyers, often returning World War II veterans, could choose from six different home models. Levitt built 17,311 homes in Bucks County, but every one was either a Levittowner, a Rancher, a Jubilee, a Pennsylvanian, a Colonial or a Country Clubber.

The original Levitttowners, as residents were called in the '50s, were expected to follow rules and regulations, such as no fences, no more than two households pets and no hanging clothes out to dry on Sundays.

Trevose, greener and wilder, was a jumble of attractive, newish houses like the Abts', boxier shingled homes from the '30s and '40s and tiny charmers that started out life as vacation cottages for Philadelphians past. The blocks were already set by the time the Bensalem Township Zoning Board was created in 1956, so an auto salvage yard sidled up to an attractive hip-roofed two-story home.

★★★

Interest in the Abt case seemed to grow after the Vogenberger murders. Suddenly, anyone who was an Abt or knew an Abt or had a sliver of new information about the investigation was sought after. At least two girls told reporters they were Kathy's best friend, and two boys anointed themselves Johnny's.

One man, a former Marine, said he was in the know thanks to his neighbor, another former Marine who worked on the Middletown Township police force. He said had to keep mum about it, though. "My neighbor was keeping me informed. I was hearing things in strict confidence," he recalled. "It would be a secret. I couldn't discuss it with anyone, or he wouldn't be able to tell me anything else."

Bensalem officers said everyone who knew they were with the police department had something to say about the killings. "You'd just have to say, 'Yeah, it's terrible,'" one said.

When Michael went out to bars, he occasionally met people who said they knew Michael Abt. People he never saw before were telling him about himself.

The week the Abt sons got their house back, I began stopping there daily so I didn't miss any news. The police chief wasn't inclined to give me any information, and the Abts' house was on my way home from the newsroom, so I'd check in with Michael and his friends, or with Clifford, whenever he was there, to see what the police had told them.

CHAPTER 11

Midnight Call from a Killer

Nothing in journalism school prepares you for two men holding guns on you.

My tension with the chief started a year earlier when the first Bensalem Township police officer was killed on duty. Patrolman Jimmy Armstrong, a well-liked 27-year-old Vietnam veteran, was shot to death by a small-time robber named Joe Hennessey. Hennessey went on the run. A five-state manhunt followed. It was one of the biggest crime stories in Philadelphia for three weeks.

Searching for a new angle one night, my colleague Ellie Reader and I walked Hennessey's Northeast Philadelphia neighborhood. I handed out my business cards with my home phone scribbled on the back. I never thought that would land me in hot water with the police chief. Through a series of random events, it did.

I had already caught the chief's attention without meaning to when I visited the apartment complex where Hennessey's girlfriend, Sheila Carr, lived. Carr worked as a "cowgal" at a Western-themed restaurant where servers wore brief cowgirl costumes and a cap gun-toting hostess fired two shots into the air as customers took their seats. I hoped I could catch Carr at home and interview her about how your life tilts when your boyfriend is the subject of a five-state manhunt.

When I walked down the steep steps to her basement apartment, I didn't know she was already on the lam with Hennessey. I knocked on the door. There was no answer. Suddenly, the door flew open. Two men were pointing guns at me. One was standing. The other was lying flat across the carpet. They ordered me into the apartment.

Nothing in journalism school prepares you for two men holding guns on you. Calculating I was safer in the hallway than inside with them, I took a baby step backward. Options flooded my mind. The men looked nice enough, except for the guns. I glanced up the stairs I had just come down, calculating whether I should try to run back up. Would they really shoot me inside an apartment building in broad daylight? Then, I heard one of them say, "Kathy, we're Bensalem police."

I was so relieved that I wobbled into the apartment and sunk into Sheila Carr's sofa. I could hear one of the officers calling the police station from the kitchen wall phone. He correctly reported that I had only knocked, and I hadn't turned the doorknob. They let me go.

As I drove back to the newsroom, I realized the officers probably had no idea it was just a reporter on the other side of the door when they flung it open. They were staking out an apartment where an armed fugitive could have turned the doorknob at any minute. They were probably as relieved as I was.

One of the people I spoke to in Hennessey's neighborhood must have passed my business card on to him. He began phoning me from different cities while he was on the run. The first time was surrealistic. After that, I always knew it was him because he used the same out-of-date phrases each time—"dig it" and "keep the faith" and "is the Pope Catholic?"

He told me he was willing to surrender to police. Would I walk with him so he wouldn't be shot? I wasn't sure which of us was less popular with the police chief, but I agreed to do it for the story.

He sounded jittery, even scared. The idea of him using me as a human shield flashed across my mind for just a second. It seemed ironic that a man who thought nothing of shooting someone else would be so terrified that someone would shoot him.

The chief and the district attorney had agreed to meet Hennessey one-on-one at a local tavern. I would be Hennessey's reluctant plus-one.

More than an hour before the surrender, Hennessey talked an old high school buddy into driving past the meet site to see if the police chief and the district attorney were being straight with him. Hennessey scrooched down on the floor of the guy's car. They spotted heads behind cars in the parking lot. Spooked, Hennessey called off the surrender.

By the time he nixed it, I was already on my way to the neighborhood bar where we planned to meet for the drive to the surrender site. Nobody had a cell phone then.

My city editor had approved my part in Hennessey's surrender, but, as I was grabbing my notebook and purse to leave the newsroom for the meetup, she circled back to my desk. She told me a more senior editor had assigned two male reporters to follow me. She suggested I duck out the back door while they were still talking, so I could lose them. They didn't know the address of the bar.

I tore out of the newspaper parking lot and headed to the address Hennessey had given me. En route, I passed the tavern where Hennessey agreed to surrender. The police chief and the district attorney were standing in front of the place. Just like Hennessey's friend, I spotted heads behind the parked cars. It all happened fast, but I was about 40 percent sure I saw someone on the roof holding a rifle. I kept driving toward the small neighborhood bar where I was expecting to meet Hennessey ready to surrender.

A clean-cut man in a T-shirt and jeans approached me as soon as I arrived. He asked if I was waiting for Joe. When I said yes, he asked if I was tape recording him. I handed him my purse and let him look through it. He asked what I saw when I drove past the surrender site. I told him about the heads behind the cars. He seemed to relax.

As we took stools at the bar, he told me he went to high school with "Joe." In a low voice, he said he and his wife heard a knock at their door a couple nights earlier and they found him standing on their porch. By then, he was all over television. They didn't want him there, but they let him in. They were hoping he could surrender before they got in trouble, but he freaked when he saw the police in the parking lot.

I used the pay phone on the barroom wall to call my editor, who would become the maid of honor at my wedding three years later. I told her I met with someone, but I couldn't say whom until I returned to the newsroom. I didn't want anyone in the cramped bar to overhear. I felt sorry for the guy and his wife.

When I got back to the newsroom, the late afternoon edition was already out. I was astonished to see the headline splashed across the front page: "Reporter Meets with Hennessey." For a second, I wondered if one of the male reporters had somehow met with Hennessey while I was at the bar.

Then I quickly scanned the story and saw my name. I couldn't move for about 30 seconds. I was so stunned I didn't even ask my friend why she wrote that. I just walked to my phone to call Chief Michaels and tell him it wasn't true. I guess he didn't believe it, because a few days later he threatened to arrest me for aiding and abetting.

My editor really thought I did meet Hennessey. She thought I was just reluctant to say his name inside the bar. It was an unfortunate miscommunication that would dog me for decades.

The newspaper ran a one-column correction the next day with the headline, "It wasn't Hennessey." The headline was smaller than the one they use for the daily bridge column in the back of the lifestyle section. I doubt anyone saw it. It didn't help me any.

The truth was I never laid eyes on Hennessey until he came to court. He did keep calling me while he was on the run, though. After I wrote about the first call, two FBI agents showed up at my desk in the newsroom. They wanted my permission to tap my home phone. I refused. Then a top editor pressured me to agree. When I wouldn't, word got around that I was going to be fired. I drove to my parents' house in New Jersey that night to tell them there was a chance I might have to move back into my old room.

I walked into the newsroom the next day prepared to be axed, but Phil Weck, the editorial editor who delivered "newscasts" to the Rotarians, saved the day. I opened the paper to see the lead editorial was about me. Phil had written that I had acted "in the best traditions of journalism" by protecting my source, no matter who that source was. I was grateful and relieved. I loved my job.

Hennessey kept calling me. One night I was asleep in my cabin in the woods when the phone rang after midnight. I fumbled for the receiver in the dark, scared something had happened to my parents. When I got it to my ear, a voice said, "This is Joe." No greeting. No apology for the late hour. Just, "This is Joe." Still half asleep, I said, "Joe who?" He identified himself as Joe Hennessey. I said something like, "For real?" He said, "Does a chicken have lips?" I remember that clearly because I'm afraid of birds. I said, "How should I know?" Seconds later, I was reaching for the lamp switch and scrambling for a pen and paper because I recognized his voice.

While Hennessey's whereabouts were the biggest story in Bucks County, I went to a house party with a friend and experienced a real fly-on-the-wall moment. I didn't know anyone there except the friend who brought me. The talk turned to Hennessey, and people started complaining about "that girl reporter" who supposedly met with him.

Hennessey's life on the lam ended weeks later. He was lured into a police net by an attractive 17-year-old blonde. At the sensational murder trial that followed, his wife, Nancy, and his girlfriend, Sheila Carr, chatted amiably in the corridors. Both women were conspicuously pregnant.

Two years after Hennessey's trial, Mike Renshaw, a *Courier Times* reporter who wrote screenplays as a side gig, walked up to my desk in the newsroom. He offhandedly told me he wrote a script idea about me and Hennessey for a new television legal drama called *Rosetti and Ryan*. "I hope you don't mind," he said, "but I made you pregnant by Hennessey." Because Renshaw was one of the funniest people I've ever known, I'm still not sure if he was kidding.

The script would have been a shoo-in, because one of the show writers was Steven de Souza, Renshaw's writing partner. Luckily for me, *Rosetti and Ryan* was cancelled after seven episodes.

Ten years later, de Souza was one of the writers on the hit movie *Die Hard*.

CHAPTER 12

Chance Favors the Detectives

> "When you're doing these neighborhood interviews, people are usually asking the cops a lot of questions about what happened, but I don't remember him being very inquisitive. After you do enough of these interviews, the strange things kind of pop out at you. He just didn't ask a lot of questions."
>
> —DETECTIVE BOB ECKERT

Ted Zajac could have passed for a '70s television detective with aviator sunglasses, three-piece suits and brown side-swept hair. He had been with the department since he worked as a civilian dispatcher in high school. His father was a township politician. After a stint in the Navy on aircraft carriers, he returned to Bensalem as a patrolman in 1961. Ten years later, he was lieutenant of detectives. His wife, Pat, said he had a knack for knowing if someone was telling the truth, even in social situations. "I'd say, 'Oh, he's a nice guy,' and he'd say, 'No. There's something about that guy. He's just not right,'" she said. "It usually turned out that Ted was right."

Often, he'd come home from work and tell her, "I know who did it. We've just got to prove it." As the Abt investigation progressed, he started to feel that way about George Geschwendt of 3722 Fleetwood Avenue.

Every morning, Zajac's office was brimming with detectives waiting to pass on information. He held morning meetings where each officer working the case shared a *Reader's Digest* version of whatever he had developed the previous day. Zajac ran the room. Based on the new leads, he came up with assignments for the day ahead. The meetings guaranteed the township detectives and the county detectives and any state troopers working the case all heard the same, most up-to-date information before they started their shifts. A lopsided number of leads focused on Clifford Abt's associates.

Zajac was hyper-focused on the murders. He didn't give press conferences. He didn't take time to read the news stories on the case. Often, he'd forget to eat.

Police dispatchers really get to know the detectives' work habits because they funnel every call that comes into the station, and they see who ducks calls. Zajac didn't duck.

"I had a very good impression of Ted from early on because of his willingness to work," said Detective Eckert, who started out as a dispatcher. "The guy would take any call. He worked hard. He wanted to make sure everything was done the best way he could. He would go over things many times to make sure they were done correctly."

Patrolman Bill Fox, another officer who started out as a dispatcher, said the lieutenant would never back off a case. He went at it full force.

Zajac figured people who violate the law in one area often will violate it in other areas, too. Thinking that a false stolen gun report just might point to the killer, he assigned an officer to sift through a wide drawer of stolen gun reports. They were printed on featherweight onion skin paper. The search yielded 15 residents who had reported guns stolen—two women and 13 men. One of the men was a mousy community college graduate named George Geschwendt.

Geschwendt had reported his .22-caliber Strum Ruger pistol stolen at 1:30 p.m. on March 5, just 90 minutes after he bought it. That sounded dodgy.

The Abts were shot with a .22-caliber pistol. The murder weapon would have to be capable of firing standard .22-caliber rounds and much more powerful .22-caliber hollow point loads. Geschwendt's Strum Ruger could.

The clincher was that Geschwendt lived across the street from the Abts. Zajac liked Geschwendt for it—at least on paper.

He wasn't the first officer to think there was something hinky about Geschwendt. Even before the victims' bodies went into rigor, Detective

Eckert thought something was off with him. The Geschwendt house was one of the first places detectives went on the night of the murders because the white Cape Cod sat across the street from the Abt house and had a good view of the property. Detective Eckert interviewed Geschwendt's mother and stepfather in their small living room. Neither had much to say. As the interview was wrapping up, the detective casually asked if anyone else lived in the house. They said, "Yeah, our son."

At that very moment, a door fell open, and Geschwendt entered the room from a bedroom whose window looked directly out at the Abt house. He was painfully thin, wearing a little white undershirt and pants. Eckert asked him the same question that he had just asked his parents. Did he notice anything out of the ordinary?

"He struck me as being a bit odd," Eckert recalled. "For one thing, people usually get excited when they're talking to a cop, but Geschwendt seemed a little down. When you're doing these neighborhood interviews, people are usually asking the cops a lot of questions about what happened, but I don't remember him being very inquisitive. After you do enough of these interviews, the strange things kind of pop out at you. He just didn't ask a lot of questions."

Sergeant William Johnson, the desk officer who took the stolen gun report, had called Geschwendt an idiot to his face. The slightly built 24-year-old had told the sergeant he left his new pistol in the saddlebag of his Honda motorcycle while he checked out what was playing at Neshaminy Mall's twin theater and wandered through Space Port, the video arcade there. He said he returned to his motorcycle to find his saddlebag straps undone and his gun missing.

Sergeant Johnson, who had a reputation for telling it like it is, said, "Only an idiot would leave a gun in the saddlebag of a motorcycle when he went shopping in the mall." Geschwendt, who always turned red at the slightest embarrassment, said he was only gone for 10 minutes, and it was the first time he had ever had anything stolen out of his saddlebag.

The sergeant was right to be suspicious. Geschwendt's gun was actually hidden away at his mother's house, and he planned to take some target practice with it in the woods that afternoon.

The stolen gun report probably seemed like a smart preemptive move on the unseasonably warm afternoon of Friday, March 5. It was reasonable to expect it would cover him if police started thumbing through gun records. Instead, it became his undoing.

Zajac brought Geschwendt into the station for questioning early on. From the first interview, the lieutenant was leery, but Chief Michaels didn't think much of him as a murder suspect.

The chief couldn't fathom why this shy, polite college grad who didn't smoke, drink or take drugs would be daydreaming about killing his neighbors. He said some things did line up right with Geschwendt, but his instincts led him to believe he was a bad candidate.

He guessed there was faint chance this painfully shy 24-year-old got face-to-face with six victims and dominated them, especially the three male victims, every one far more muscular than he. To the chief, Geschwendt just didn't seem like murderer material. After all, he was so mild-mannered that a hiring manager had turned him down for a job a few days earlier because he didn't seem assertive enough.

Besides, from the get-go, Chief Michaels told reporters he had a gut feeling the killer or killers were not acquainted with the Abts. He just didn't believe anyone who knew the Abts would have shot their dog.

Zajac still thought the timid man was hiding something. As the chief put it later, "Teddy was warm for him."

Despite what his superior officer said, George Geschwendt's name had already been moved to the A-list in the back of Zajac's mind.

Although Geschwendt didn't know it then, as far as the lead detective was concerned, he had entered the limbo between person of interest and defendant.

While some officers chased stories of Clifford Abt's drug connections, Zajac and others kept chasing their hunches about Geschwendt, but they needed hard evidence.

Thinking a polygraph exam might tip something, Zajac sent two detectives to pick up Geschwendt at his home on the evening of March 17, several hours after the Abts' funeral. Geschwendt didn't seem to have any misgivings as he ducked into the back seat of the two-door detective car, but the conversation lagged on the three-mile drive to the station. One of the detectives noticed Geschwendt looked dressed up, so he asked if he had attended the Abt funeral earlier that day. Geschwendt said no. He told them he was out of work and looking for a job. He was dressed for an interview at an employment agency.

Detectives joke that you don't always need a polygraph to tell if a suspect is lying. Detective Eckert gave an example: "If you're interviewing them and you ask, 'What kind of sentence do you think someone should get for this,' a guilty guy's going to say, 'Oh, I wouldn't give much for this.'"

When Geschwendt got to the station, Zajac was waiting for him, along with a police officer who had attended polygraph classes. Geschwendt reportedly was the officer's eleventh subject.

Several detectives who thought Zajac was on to something milled around outside the small interview room. They waited expectantly, certain Geschwendt would walk out in bracelets.

He topped all their mental lists of likely suspects. First, there was something off about him. Second, he reported a gun of the correct caliber stolen 90 minutes after he bought it. Third, he lived across the street from the victims. It added up.

Police interrogations switched from hard knocks to soft sell after the 1964 Miranda decision that protected the rights of suspects. Zajac was a new breed of interrogator. He put subjects at ease with a smile or a head nod. He gave you the feeling he understood you without ever actually saying he did. He listened more than he talked. As Chief Michaels put it, "There are certain people who are endowed with the ability to talk. It's not merely the gift of gab. It's the ability to get through to people. Fortunately, Teddy is one."

The polygraph examiner hooked Geschwendt up, and they matter-of-factly lobbed questions at him: Were you off your property anytime Friday? Do you resent being asked to take a lie detector test?

The first question to move the needle was, "Was your gun actually stolen?"

It jumped again when the polygraph operator said two victims had rags stuffed in their mouths and then read the names aloud. The only people who would recognize the correct names were the killer, the police and the medical examiner.

The most consequential question never moved the needle, though: "Regarding the incident Friday night at the Abt house, are you yourself responsible for that?

Zajac showed Geschwendt a .22-caliber handgun and asked if it looked like his stolen gun. Geschwendt stared for a second. Then he said the fine pattern on the grip was different. Zajac didn't challenge him, but he made a mental note that Geschwendt said he owned the gun for only 90 minutes, and it was in his saddlebag most of that time, yet he could recall the small pattern on the grip nine days later. He got the feeling the guy wasn't leveling with him.

The officers outside the interview room were baffled when Geschwendt walked out of the interview room with his hands uncuffed.

"We were all in the building waiting. We thought they were going to crack him. They're going to get him to admit it," Detective Eckert said. "When that didn't happen, I was thinking, 'What? The guy did it. There's no way around it. How come he's not hitting on it?'"

Then someone realized the question was flubbed. The needle never budged because Geschwendt honestly believed he was not responsible for the deaths. He thought the Abts were responsible for their own deaths, even 12-year-old Kathy. In his mind, they deserved to die.

"We were all disappointed. It really set people back on their heels a bit," Detective Eckert said.

Detective Bill Edwards, the evidence technician who usually left his work problems at the office, was still dismayed when he got home that night. "I know he did it," he told his wife Lucy.

Zajac could draw a line from Geschwendt to the crimes, but it wasn't a very thick line. In fact, it was threadlike.

Detectives were hoping to hitch Geschwendt to the murders, but they had no fingerprints and no smoking gun. They were getting no closer to an arrest until two things happened.

First, Geschwendt fouled up. Police didn't have a smoking gun, but they did get a muddy one. Two boys were fishing along the gray bank of the Neshaminy Creek when they spotted several odd items that appeared to have been tossed from the riverbank or the bridge overhead. Adam Laster and Michael Scher spotted a .22-caliber pistol half in and half out of the creek. The grip was stuck in the muck. Scher pulled the gun out and unloaded its six bullets. He placed the Strum Ruger in his tackle box. When he got home, he showed it to his stepfather, who, in turn, brought it to the Lower Southampton Police Department.

Bensalem and Lower Southampton bump on the map. Their police stations are just miles apart. Unfortunately, there were no computerized lists of recovered guns in 1976, so the murder weapon on the Bensalem detectives' wish list was parked in a locker in Lower Southampton, unbeknownst to police from both jurisdictions.

Then Bensalem Police got a lucky break. By chance, a Bensalem officer and a Lower Southampton officer both stopped for coffee in the backroom of the Trevose Fire Company, a mile from the murder scene. A random conversation turned to the missing gun. The Lower South officer mentioned a kid had found a gun under a bridge about three miles from the Abt house. It was in a locker at the police station. It could be the murder weapon. A quick check of the serial number revealed it was a match.

★★★

After pulling off a risky 11-hour murder spree without a glitch, Geschwendt tripped himself up by failing to properly dispose of his gun. Screwups happen often. Son of Sam killer David Berkowitz was brought down because he parked his cream-colored Ford Galaxie in front of a fire hydrant. Ted Bundy, who left a trail of bodies across the country, was foiled when a Pensacola patrolman spotted him driving a bright orange Volkswagen Beetle that had been reported stolen. BTK killer Dennis Rader sent a Wichita television station a floppy disk with hidden metadata that led straight back to him. After reputed boy geniuses Nathan Leopold and Richard Loeb bludgeoned 14-year-old Bobby Franks in the case that rocked Chicago in 1924, they did themselves in by accidentally dropping Leopold's expensive prescription eyeglasses next to the body.

***

The Bensalem station was abuzz as word got out that the murder weapon was in the house. Suddenly, the Abt investigation had legs.

Three officers were dispatched to the exact spot where the gun was found. They found seven spent .22 magnum shells and a skinny metal headband with ear protectors on either end. The items appeared to have been tossed from atop the busy Brownsville Road bridge overhead. It was a major break in the case. Detective Eckert made a sketch of the area. Detective David Stiles took black-and-white aerial photographs.

Chance went against Geschwendt twice. First, he missed his mark ditching the gun, so it landed on the creek bank instead of the creek bottom. Then, an offhand conversation at a cafeteria table in the back room of a firehouse led police to his Ruger.

"It really was a miracle that the gun didn't land in the deep water, because they probably never would have found it," Officer Clee said. "And, if those cops never had that conversation, I don't know what the hell would have happened."

The discovery sent the investigation spinning in a new direction. The drug theory that had taken so much police time was kaput. The new probable suspect was the Abt boys' childhood friend George Geschwendt. Their homes faced each other.

CHAPTER 13

Friday's Child

When a news reporter called George Geschwendt's college adviser for comment after his arrest for six grisly murders, the adviser couldn't recall the name.

George was Friday's child. He was born on Friday, September 7, 1951, to Josephine and Fred Geschwendt Sr. Friday's child, according to the nursery rhyme, is loving and giving.

Most Friday's children don't come home to an alcoholic father who goes after them with knives, though. George's dismal childhood would have been a major clue for investigators if anyone outside his home knew about it. The family of six was buttoned up, though. To say they kept their problems to themselves would be an understatement. They didn't even talk among themselves.

George was the youngest of four children in a home where the father ate first, and his wife and children lived on his scraps.

Fred Geschwendt Sr. was a brutal alcoholic who once tried to mow his four children down with his car.

He beat his wife, cursed her in German, and called her a "whore" and a "Pollock bitch" in front of their young children. He threw her new vacuum cleaner out of a window. He upbraided her whenever she tried to do things for George when he was a toddler. One Christmas, he broke the children's presents. Another time, he threw their clothes out a window. He went after his older son with a knife, and the boy jumped out a window to save himself.

He never kissed his children or sat them on his lap. He never discussed anything with them. The only conversation allowed in the house was a yes or no answer to his questions.

Josephine Geschwendt became chronically nervous long before her husband left her when George was five. Locked in her own anxiety, she never attended a PTA meeting, met with one of George's teachers or signed her son up for after-school activities. Neighbors, unaware of what was going on inside the small white house, just pegged her as aloof.

George's life completely turned around in 1963 when Clifford Abt, 12, and his younger brother, Michael, moved across the street. The Abt family was as playful and extroverted as his was anxious and introverted. Suddenly, George was exploring the woods and wading in the creek. Boys suddenly huddled around the ancient basketball hoop on his garage.

When they were still in middle school, Clifford and George tossed some rocks through the windows of a home they thought was abandoned. It was not. One stone narrowly missed a sleeping baby. The mother called George's mother to complain.

Then the boys dragged rocks and lumber across the railroad tracks that crisscrossed the woods where they played. A railroad man discovered the mischief in the nick of time before a train was derailed, but George and Clifford and two other boys were nabbed. When George's mother had to pay $212.50 in restitution, more than a week's pay, his horsing around was kaput. She nipped George's friendships in the bud. She ordered him to stay away from the Abts and the other boys.

Just like police learn something from every case they work, or a mechanic recalls an errant sound that tips him off to a certain problem, reporters learn something from almost every story they report. I learned to assume nothing when Clifford told me the incident that angered Geschwendt's mother was "kid shit." I thought they stole apples or knocked a baseball through a picture window and ran away because that's the worst thing kids in my small town did.

It wasn't in my experience to nearly bean a baby with a rock or to come minutes away from derailing a train. Without knowing the details,

I just tagged Mrs. Geschwendt as a very strict mother. Actually, she had to pay the equivalent of $1,100 in today's dollars for George's transgression, and she had to do it on a hotel cleaner's salary.

After that, I learned to ask follow-up questions.

Michael, who was 11 when the train incident occurred, was too young to understand everything that transpired, but he did notice George abruptly vanished from their lives. "That was the last we saw of George forever, unless we saw him at school," he said.

Once again, George's life completely turned around, this time for the worse. With no close friends as he entered high school, he became withdrawn and detached.

His mother had remarried. Fautino "Tino" Colon, her new husband, was a friendly man with a thick accent who had emigrated from Puerto Rico. George had little relationship with him. The six family members lived under the same roof, but they rarely discussed anything.

George kept to himself. He showed little animation for a teenager. He quit making eye contact.

He sat in the front row of the school bus with a stack of books next to him. One girl who rode the bus thought the books may have served as a protective barrier because boys on the bus called George names. The girl tried to talk with him, but all she could ever get out of him was a yes or no answer.

A male classmate, who described himself as someone who likes to talk, sat behind George in one class, but he doesn't think they exchanged more than 10 words all year.

Geschwendt later told a psychologist he spent most of his school hours daydreaming.

Although he had a slightly above average IQ, he was a C student at Bensalem High School, graduating 170th out of the 328 students in his class. He took no advanced classes. He had no close friends. He never dated a girl. He had no self-confidence. He didn't like the sound of his own voice.

A series of unconnected things had gone wrong to get George to the precipice where he decided to murder a family. First, his mother cut off his friendship with the Abts. A shearing-machine accident cut off half his middle finger and the tips of two others, so he became embarrassed to show his right hand. He rarely gestured. He sat with his hands folded one over the other. By high school, he was a classic loner living across the street from three popular, outgoing teenagers whose world was closed to him.

The six lines of type beneath his photo in the 1970 Bensalem High Yearbook betrayed none of that, though. His yearbook entry painted George simply as a senior who liked swimming and driving cars. His favorite food was chili con carne. His ambition was to join the Navy. His pet peeves were school and cold weather. His nickname was "Gesch."

He did join the Navy after high school, but he didn't get the assignment he wanted. And he learned too late that he was ill-suited for a life on the water because he was prone to seasickness. He tried going AWOL, but his mother and stepfather talked him into turning himself in. He was busted one rank upon his return. By then, he really wanted out of his six-year enlistment, so he confessed to using marijuana, methamphetamine and LSD. None of it was true. He never used drugs.

He managed to leave the Navy four years early without being tagged with a dishonorable discharge. After he washed out, he used his veterans benefits to enroll at Bucks County Community College, where he was a C student again. A classmate said the only thing that made him stand out was the motorcycle helmet he always carried. When a news reporter called his college adviser for comment after his arrest for six grisly murders, the adviser couldn't recall the name.

Geschwendt earned an associate degree in business administration, but he didn't interview well, and he couldn't get a job in his field. He enrolled at a truck driving school in Arizona, but the teachers were bad, the tires were bald and the job he hoped for never materialized despite the advertisements that promised 90 percent of the graduates got work.

His dream was to move to Florida, but he never had the money. He drifted from job to job. He worked for a burial service. He was a telephone solicitor. A former employer said he always had dreams of doing things he couldn't do. A woman hired him as a landscaper because she felt sorry for him. The landscaping job was seasonal. When he lost it at the end of the summer of '75, he went on public assistance.

Everything he wanted seemed just out of reach—a decent job, money for Florida and one more thing. He wanted his old friendship with the Abts.

Instead, he said, the Abts tormented him. One day in November of 1975, he found trash in front of his house. When he went out to pick it up, he believed he could hear the Abts at their windows looking and laughing. Whether they were actually in the window or just in his mind, the incident started the clock.

The idea of killing took root in Geschwendt's mind. He made the decision to save his public assistance checks to buy a gun. He did not "snap." He planned the murders for four months.

His ticking clock was already at quarter-past when he ran into Michael and two of his friends in front of his house on Christmas morning in 1975. The young men wished him a merry Christmas. His response fuddled them. It was like talking to a zombie, Michael said.

"All three of us looked at each other, but we didn't say a word until we got inside the house. Then we all said the same thing: 'What the fuck is wrong with that guy?'" Michael said. "It didn't take a clinical psychiatrist to see there was something wrong. Now this is the Christmas right before he killed my family."

All three men were taken aback by Geschwendt's mannerisms, but none spotted the malevolence lurking beneath the surface. Even after the mass murder, none of them suspected Geschwendt. The mass murderer Trevose residents carried around in their imaginations was neither submissive nor scrawny. He was scary.

★★★

Ten weeks after that Christmas encounter, Geschwendt walked out of Jay's Guns and Shooting Supply in Levittown with two boxes of ammunition, and a leather holster made to slide onto a belt and a brand-new .22-caliber Ruger that cost him $96.50. The gun came with an instruction booklet, but Jay Scheidecker, the store owner, had to show Geschwendt how to change the cartridge.

Ninety minutes after that, the newly minted serial killer walked into the Bensalem Township Police Station to tell Sergeant Johnson his gun was stolen. It wasn't.

After he left the police station, Geschwendt rode his motorcycle into a thick woods near his house where he practiced firing rounds into an abandoned truck. Seven days later, he was firing it for real. He thought he had a foolproof plan. He didn't.

On March 22, detectives Bob Eckert and Tom Scaricaciottoli visited Geschwendt's brother's workplace, hoping to interview him. Fred Geschwendt Jr. was out on the road when they arrived, but his boss W. H. Jaxheimer Jr. confirmed that Fred was at work until around 5:30 p.m. on the day the Abts were killed. Then Jaxheimer recalled a crack that Fred made when he came to work the next day. Fred mentioned there had been a mobile crime lab parked in front of his house the previous night. He casually remarked that the kid who lived across the street was probably in trouble again.

The detectives were putting big pieces together, but, at about 4:30 p.m. that afternoon, Chief Michaels told reporters there was nothing new.

Geschwendt may have been marveling that he hadn't been caught 10 days after the slayings, but, within hours, both his life and his story would come apart.

CHAPTER 14

The Polygraph Virtuoso

> "If George had kept his mouth shut, he probably could have gotten away with the whole thing."
>
> —PATROLMAN DAVE CLEE

Around dinnertime, Detectives Ed Keyser and Norm Martin were detailed to pick Geschwendt up at his home. The district attorney's office was involved every step of the way because police wanted an arrest that would stand up in court. An assistant DA recommended that the detectives leave the premises immediately if Geschwendt would not go with them willingly.

The detectives knocked on the door. Geschwendt answered. They stood on the exterior side of the threshold and introduced themselves. Oddly, Geschwendt said, "Step in." They told him they would like him to come to headquarters because they wanted to obtain some information from him.

He didn't show much reluctance about riding to the police station, but he did ask what they wanted to talk to him about. Not wanting to tip him off, they said they'd like to go over anything he might have seen on the night the incident took place. He agreed to go. They told him they'd give him a ride back.

He was already wearing a lightweight jacket, so he just walked outside with them and climbed into the back of the two-door unmarked car that Keyser drove. There was little conversation on the way to the station because he had not yet been read his rights. They got to the station around 6:25 p.m. Evening hours are considered the Goldilocks hours to interrogate suspects because dinner breaks don't upset the flow of the interview, but the timing that night was coincidental. Things just came together then.

It was almost 8 p.m. when Geschwendt faced off across a table with Zajac and a polygraph examiner again. This time around, Geschwendt was eye-to-eye with a polygraph virtuoso named Dick Batezel. One defense attorney called Batezel one of the best of the best.

With his crewcut, sunglasses, short-sleeved white shirts and ties and the ever-present gun holstered on his belt or under his armpit, the square-shouldered father of six still looked a little like the career Marine he once was. He served two township police departments with distinction before he was plucked away to serve on the county detective squad, an arm of the DA's office. By the time he got to the county, Batezel had already had a storied career as a homicide investigator.

He worked the Mary Mamon murder case that shocked the entire country on Easter weekend in 1967. A hammer-wielding killer slipped into Mrs. Lorraine Mullery's Levittown home through an open garage door on Holy Thursday, one of the most sacred days of the year for Christians. The intruder bludgeoned Mrs. Mullery to death and chased two children around the house with a hammer.

The neighbors who spotted a stranger walking into the Mullerys' garage that morning described a heavy-set man with horn-rimmed glasses, gray trousers, a big coat and a hat with ear flaps. Police issued an artist's sketch. In an abrupt about-face, they announced the mannish-looking killer in their sketch was actually a woman. Readers followed every twist and turn in the case. There were plenty.

Mrs. Mamon, the suspect, was a female who dressed as a male. She worked as a chemist—unusual for a woman in the '60s. She was a divorced mother of four—also unusual in the '60s. Her nickname was Tarzan.

Tabloid headlines labeled her "mannish" and "a divorcee." Police described her as "a lesbian subject who looks like a man." Headline writers stopped just short of that with "Woman Ex-Athlete Held in Slaying" and "Husky Housewife Sought as Prime Murder Suspect."

Waves of shocking headlines drew readers into the stories. The well-to-do suspect slipped away before police could arrest her. She was found hiding in an Alabama convent. A background check revealed she had been acquitted of killing a five-year-old girl three decades earlier.

And, because the murder happened in Levittown, Pennsylvania, one of the country's first cookie-cutter suburbs, erroneous rumors circulated that Mrs. Mamon had intended to kill a different woman, but she became confused and entered the wrong house because all the homes on Levittown's curvilinear streets looked so much alike.

It was the most sensational case in Bucks County history—until it was surpassed by the Abt case. Batezel worked both of them.

Richard R. Fink, who would become Geschwendt's public defender, said Batezel resembled a professional jockey whenever he was gathering evidence, a jockey who stares straight ahead but takes in everything around the track as his horse moves forward. Batezel might stare at a spot on the floor as a suspect spoke or he might seem to stare straight through him as he carefully processed what he was hearing and put all the pieces together in his mind.

Batezel always treated suspects with respect. He never lied to them. He never made threats. He had no axes to grind.

Fink described him as just panning for gold when he interviewed a suspect. He'd have well-crafted questions up his sleeve to get him to the spot where the gold might collect. Then he would start digging. Like in so many other big cases he worked, this time Batezel did not disappoint.

Defense attorneys call polygraph exams "confession machines," because, when a suspect takes a polygraph and fails it, his will is broken, Fink said. He may assume the police have all the evidence they need to convict him.

Fink said Geschwendt wasn't a suspect who police could play "go fish" with because he was a community college graduate with an IQ of 113, a number that is considered "high average" or about the 80th percentile. Plus, he was totally confident he hadn't left a single fingerprint to tie him to the slayings. He was no pushover. He was no match for Batezel, though.

Batezel's first impression of Geschwendt was that he was an "introverted individual" and "no great conversationalist."

When the three men entered the small, windowless interview room, Geschwendt was unaware the next three hours would be life changing for him. As he took his seat, he was probably optimistic he could beat the polygraph as he had five days earlier. Zajac and Batezel had other plans. They knew whodunnit, but they needed to know why, and they needed a signed confession.

The interview room was designed to eliminate distractions. There was one desk and some chairs. An exhaust fan whirred overhead. The walls were dark-brown faux wood paneling. The only light source was a set of fluorescent tube lights that shone through plastic panels in the ceiling.

The detectives told Geschwendt certain matters had developed, and they would like to question him further if he had no objections. He said he didn't mind.

They handed him a Miranda form informing him of his rights, including the right to have an attorney present. He asked if it was the same form he had signed the first time. They told him it was, but they wanted him to read it again. They didn't want to skirt the law. He took about 90 seconds to read it. Then he signed it. They asked if he understood everything on the form. He said he did.

"Do you want to answer our questions without a lawyer being present to represent you?" Detective Batezel asked him.

"I am not sure," he answered. "Would it make any difference?"

"That's strictly up to you, George," Batezel said, aware his every word would matter when the case came to court.

"Well, I want to tell the truth," Geschwendt lied.

"Do you want to tell us what you told us earlier?" Lieutenant Zajac said.

"Yes," he said.

"Do you want to answer our questions without a lawyer being present to represent you?" Zajac asked.

"Well," Geschwendt stuttered, "Maybe I ought to have a lawyer. Well, if I had a lawyer here to represent me, would I get to talk to him before I would answer any questions?"

"Would you repeat the question?" Zajac stalled.

"I said if I had a lawyer, would I get to talk to him before I answered the questions for you?" Geschwendt asked.

"However you want to do it, George," Zajac said. "All we are going to do is ask you exactly what you told us the first time. Now, do you want to answer our questions without a lawyer being present?"

Geschwendt agreed to answer the questions. As soon as he was hooked up to the polygraph, they told him his gun had been found. The revelation must have hit him like a thunderclap. It was too late, though. He was already hooked up.

They asked him if he knew where they had found it. He said no. Suddenly, he was on unsure footing.

He asked why they didn't tell him they found the gun. Ignoring his question, they told him his gun was already at the FBI lab in Washington.

Their questions started coming at a faster clip: "Were you off your property at any time on Friday?"

They popped out a new, improved version of the direct question the other examiner had asked on March 17: "Did you fire one or more of the shots that resulted in the deaths of the people in the Abt house?"

Batezel lobbed questions at him in a known-solution, peak-of-tension format. The examiner asks five to nine nearly identical yes-or-no questions to suss out what the suspect knows about the crime. One question includes something only the guilty party and the police know.

The examiner keeps an eye on the suspect's heart rate, respiration, blood pressure and skin response when he hears that question. The killer knows the question is coming, and he becomes unnerved waiting for it.

Batezel asked Geschwendt:

If you disposed of that .22 revolver, was it in:

P. Neshaminy Creek at Old Lincoln Highway
Q. Neshaminy Creek at Route 1
R. Neshaminy Creek at Bridgetown Pike
S. Neshaminy Creek at Brownsville Road
T. Neshaminy Creek at Second Street Pike
U. Neshaminy Creek at Bustleton Pike
V. Neshaminy Creek at Bristol Road
W. Neshaminy Creek at Worthington Mill Road

Geschwendt answered with a litany of "nos," but the letter "S" plainly made the polygraph needle jump.

The questions kept coming in Batezel's respectful monotone:

If you threw or placed anything on the bodies,

A. Would that be a shovel?

B. Would that be a rake?

C. Would that be a broom?

D. Would that be a tire?

E. Would that be a bike?

F. Would that be a chair?

G. Would that be a ladder?

H. Would that be a wheelbarrow?

When Batezel mentioned the tire that topped Gary Engle's body, the needle hopped enough to be noticed even by an untrained eye. Without any doubt, Geschwendt knew a tire had been tossed over Engle's body.

Finally, they advised Geschwendt that there was a problem with the polygraph. He asked what they meant. They told him in plain words that he flunked.

Suddenly adrift, he asked to see the polygraph chart to see where it showed he was lying. Batezel scotched that.

Geschwendt was no chump. He tried to get them into a discussion about how the machine could know he was lying.

They told him they knew he was the one who committed the murders, and they just wanted to know why.

Again, he asked to see the evidence that he was lying. He asked a total of 10 times. They told him he would see it at his murder trial.

They said only the person who had killed the Abts would know what item was placed on top of Gary's body, and his responses showed he knew it was a tire. Without any doubt, they said, he knew what the body had been covered with. Fudging, he said he probably reacted because he had dropped a tire on his foot recently. He knew he was in a tight spot.

Even after he failed the test conclusively, Geschwendt was too smart to confess. He asked how the machine could know he was lying. He must have sensed he was in over his head. He asked if they had any fingerprints. He asked to see the evidence again and again.

The detectives knew the gun was the only evidence they had. They had no witnesses, no hairs and, thanks to Geschwendt's dishwashing gloves, no fingerprints. They needed a confession to make their case, so they pressed on.

Bluffing, they asked how he would explain it if one of his head hairs was found at the Abt house. He thought fast. He proposed a cockamamie scenario: maybe one of his hairs fell on the barrel when he bought his gun and then maybe whoever stole his gun also killed the Abts, and maybe his hair dropped off the barrel inside the Abt house when the real killer fired the gun.

Batezel asked if he didn't think it was odd that the weapon that he bought and left unattended was stolen, and, exactly a week later, it was used to murder six people right across the street from his house.

They asked why he killed the Abts. First Zajac. Then Batezel. Then Zajac. And so on. They did it 15 or 20 times. He must have been needled.

By 10 p.m., Zajac and Batezel were certain Geschwendt murdered the Abts, but they knew they didn't have enough evidence to arrest him.

Then Batezel asked if one of the other members of the family did something to him or his family that caused him to do it.

Bingo.

Geschwendt began to open up. Admitting to doing something like that would be hard, he said.

The detectives assured him they understood.

Did one of the Abts shoot him with a BB?
Did the Abt boys challenge his masculinity?
Did he think Clifford's involvement with drugs was ruining the neighborhood?
Did the Abts' Saint Bernard chase after his motorcycle?
Did one of the Abt girls rebuff him?

Then, in a sudden about-face, Geschwendt regained his fight. He was no longer wobbly. "If you know I did this, show me the evidence," he demanded.

Again, the detectives asked why he did it.

He wanted to know what difference that would make. They said they'd like to understand what caused him to do this.

Batezel or Zajac had to find a question that would bring his defenses tumbling down. They couldn't allow him to clam up and go home.

Fink always tells his clients they don't have to worry about tough-guy detectives who threaten you and bully you and tell you how much time you're going to do and all that bullshit, because you will naturally mistrust them. He tells them it's the friendly ones who are dangerous, the ones who say they want to hear your side.

"Criminals don't confess because they like the detective," Fink said. "They don't confess to cleanse their soul. They do it because you hit their trigger and they go off. Batezel figured out exactly how to hit George's trigger."

Batezel knew the magic words to pop the balloon, Fink said. What he had up his sleeve was one softhearted question that would get all the answers rushing out of Geschwendt. He let it rip: "Oh George, what did they do to you?"

Forty-seven years after the murders, Dave Clee, who discovered the bodies, still says, "If George had kept his mouth shut, he probably could have gotten away with the whole thing."

But he didn't. He fell for it. He caved. He overshared.

He told Zajac and Batezel that he is a very sensitive person who likes to keep to himself, but the Abts wouldn't leave him alone. The killer who had terrified the suburbs for 10 days was quickly unravelling because someone had finally asked to hear his side.

"I didn't want to hurt anybody, but they made me," Geschwendt said. Punctuating his sentences with "I" and "me," he opened up to them: "I like to keep to myself. I don't bother with anybody. I am a perceptive person. I take a lot of things seriously. Everything is pretty serious to me."

He wasn't a monster; he was a perceptive person.

While Geschwendt was unfurling his confession, there was a flurry of activity inches away on the other side of the interrogation room door. Michael Kane of the DA's office was standing there listening. He didn't have his ear to the door exactly, but he could make out the voices well enough. He checked his watch. It was 10:10 p.m. on the dot.

Kane, a graduate of Duke University School of Law, didn't waste a minute. While the detectives were still listening to Geschwendt unspool his confession, Kane found a typewriter and a secretary to type up six complaints in a jiffy, each one charging Geschwendt with one of the six murders. Then he called the local district justice at home and told him to get to his office.

Meanwhile, inside the windowless interview room, the whole truth came gushing out of Geschwendt. Zajac and Batezel, with no malice and no threats, had outfoxed a spree murderer.

Zajac knew Geschwendt did it, but, like a ship's captain staring at an iceberg, he needed to see the huge icy base, the part that lay underneath, because he needed the motive to convince a jury. Geschwendt obliged.

He told them Michael and his friends called him "jerk-off" and "shithead" and "prick." Johnny shot BBs at his house and his motorcycle, he said. They made prank calls. Heidi left dung on his lawn. He hit stones with his lawnmower, and he suspected the Abts put them there. Once someone sent flowers to his house, cash on delivery. A taxicab pulled up in front of his house one day and, when he went out to talk to the cabbie, he believed he saw the Abt children at their windows laughing. He said the Abts would make their cars backfire in front of his house. His hatred of the Abts had been bubbling up inside him for four long years.

The backfires were real. They were not intended for Geschwendt, though. Jack Abt had taught his son's friends how to make their cars backfire loudly as a lark. Whenever they rode past and spotted him in his lawn chair reading his paper, they'd acknowledge him with a backfire. They were tributes of sorts, and they weren't intended for anyone on the other side of Fleetwood Avenue.

Geschwendt said he was already depressed because he couldn't find a good job despite earning a business administration degree, and so much anger had built up in his mind against the Abts for hounding him that, in November 1975, he began plotting to kill the entire family. It was actually the second time he thought of killing an entire family. The first time he considered killing his own.

He chose a .22-caliber pistol because it was much cheaper than a .38. He bought 100 rounds of regular ammunition and 50 copper-jacketed hollow-point magnum cartridges. The more expensive hollow points were advertised as more effective at rapidly incapacitating a target. He also bought a set of ear protectors. He said he was concerned that so many loud closeup shots might damage his hearing. He held the Ruger no more than a foot or two from their faces.

He said nothing he told Sergeant Johnson about the gun being stolen was true. He did ride his motorcycle to the mall, but he didn't stop. He just circled the parking lot and went home and hid the pistol. Then he jumped on his Honda and rode to police headquarters to file the theft report. That afternoon, he rode to the woods where he practiced shooting into a light-colored abandoned truck.

He kept talking. His account was detailed. As an aside, he mentioned that the whole thing probably wouldn't have happened if it weren't so easy to buy a gun.

He said he planned to kill the Abts earlier in the week, but his mother fell ill for three days. She called in sick to her job as a cleaner at the nearby Mall Motel. He knew he had to pick a day when his mother was out of the house. Friday, March 12, was her first day back on the job. As soon as she left for work, he put a note on the stove saying he was going out to look for work. Instead, he crossed the street.

He used his gun to smash the glass in the Abts' kitchen door, reached in, reversed the lock Michael had just turned, and turned the knob. He sat silently waiting for his first victim for almost seven hours until School Bus No. 50 from Neil Armstrong Middle School rolled into the neighborhood around 3:15 p.m.

Geschwendt said none of his victims had any last words because he did not give them a chance.

He didn't know how many shots he fired, but he recalled reloading several times.

He shoved Jack Abt's brawny body down the basement steps.

He didn't know exactly how many times he shot Peggy Abt, but she kept moaning, so he stuffed a rag in her mouth.

He waited behind the living room wall while Margie had a brief phone conversation. She didn't say anything to the person on the other end that would suggest she was wary. Seconds after she put the receiver back in its chrome cradle, he moved forward and shoved his gun in her face. He fired two bullets into her head and pushed her down the stairs on top of her father.

He knew the last person only as "Engle." He had never met him, but he killed him anyway, because he was a friend of the Abts.

After that, he hid in the house for another half hour waiting for Michael and Clifford to return, but the phone kept ringing and ringing. He thought the caller might be the type of person who would worry because no one was answering and contact the police and send them to the house.

He said if the phone had not been ringing, he would have waited until midnight if necessary to kill the last two. Michael was the one he wanted most.

He told the detectives that he removed his eyeglasses before he walked out the Abts' front door in case a neighbor spotted him. Instead of walking directly across the street and slipping into his own house, he circled the block first. He still wasn't certain whether someone was hiding on the Abts' second floor. If they were, the sound of the door shutting might prompt them to peek out a front window. He wanted to throw them off his trail.

When he finally got home after his nearly 11-hour killing spree, he hid his gun, gloves and clothing in his motorcycle saddlebags and locked the garage. Then he made himself a tuna fish sandwich. By the time Officer Clee discovered the carnage he left across the street, he was watching a little television with his family.

He answered a few questions for a Bensalem detective who canvassed the block after the bodies were discovered, but, by 9 p.m., he was snuggled in bed. He told the polygraph examiner that he rarely let his emotions out, so shooting six people was somewhat of a relief for him.

He slept soundly until he was awakened by a burst of police activity across the street. When he heard the cars pulling up, he got out of bed, went to the window, watched what was going on outside the Abts' for a few minutes, and then fell right back to sleep.

The next morning, he handed his mother his blood-stained gray slacks to launder. She just looked at the spots and threw them in the wash. She didn't ask him about the blood, even though detectives had visited their home the previous evening to ask about six murders directly across the street. When the pants were dry, he added them and his leather jacket to a pile his mother was dropping off at Goodwill.

That weekend he felt he had to tell someone what he did, not to get it off his chest but to brag. He told his mother, but he didn't tell her the whole truth. He said he had been forced at gunpoint to go over to the Abt house. He didn't fully confess, and she didn't push him for details. She never called the police. He always identified with his mother. They both kept their heads down and tried to get along.

Although reporters and rubberneckers swarmed the street between the Abt and Geschwendt houses that morning, when George pulled his Honda out of his garage no one noticed his black vinyl saddlebags bulging with blood-spattered size-9D boots. Not one of the dozens of people milling around talking about the murders pegged him as the source of their fears.

He steered toward Washington Crossing State Park. A half hour later, he was tossing the incriminating items into the Delaware River near the spot where George Washington made his historic crossing on Christmas Day 1776, nearly two hundred years earlier.

Three days later, he drove his mother's red Mustang to a nearby bridge. He pitched his gun, his ear protectors, the spent cartridges, and some live rounds into the fast-flowing Neshaminy Creek. At least he thought he had.

Throughout his hours of interrogation, Geschwendt showed no emotion and expressed only one regret. He was disappointed he did not kill the other two Abts.

Zajac and Batezel had clinched it. They were about to leave the interview room with the confession that would make their case when Geschwendt told them one more thing. He said he really thought they had him when they polygraphed him back on March 17.

As they walked out of the room, an officer moved forward to frisk Geschwendt. The murder suspect casually reached into his pocket, pulled out a knife and handed it over.

Kane, the assistant DA who had been listening at the door, gifted the detectives with the paperwork he had prepared. By 11:30 p.m., they were on their way to the district justice's office. They left through a back door in case the lobby was still thick with reporters.

Geschwendt was arraigned at 11:45 p.m. The district justice also signed a search warrant for his home. He handed the suspect an application for a public defender. Geschwendt was a shoo-in. He had no job. His saving account at Trevose Savings & Loan had a $15 balance. His only other asset was his Honda motorcycle worth about $600.

Geschwendt's writing on the application appeared juvenile compared with that of the other signers. His penmanship was painstaking, and his signature had none of the distinctive flourishes often added by adult men accustomed to signing documents.

When they returned to the station just past midnight, Geschwendt, who hadn't eaten for at least six hours, downed a steak sandwich and a cup of water.

The detectives were still busy working when Chief Michaels and DA Ken Biehn stepped in front of the cameras for a 12:30 a.m. press conference they called to announce the arrest.

When Geschwendt returned to Bensalem, Detective Antony Maniscola from the Middletown Township Police Department was waiting to ask him if he would mind taking a polygraph in connection with the Vogenberger murders. Geschwendt agreed. "I have nothing to lose as I did not do the crime," he said in his usual stilted language.

Maniscola remembered the prisoner seemed calm and collected, despite the late hour and his arrest. And, for a man who just confessed to killing six people and a beloved family pet, Maniscola recalled he didn't seem at all contrite.

Lieutenant Zajac decided it wouldn't be practical to fingerprint and photograph Geschwendt at the police station with reporters around and the Abts and their friends so close. Keyser and Martin, the detectives who drove Geschwendt to the police station, led the suspect out a back door. They drove him to the Bristol Township Police Department.

The new prisoner would spend his first night in lockup in a holding cell in the neighboring township. The only conversation on the 10-mile car ride was Geschwendt asking about what the police were going to do.

The thought that a killer sat silently in his unsuspecting victims' home for almost 11 hours was chilling, even to police. As Detective Eckert put it, "My God, when we thought of him sitting there all day at that piano waiting for people to come in…"

Patrolman Bill Fox, who graduated from Bensalem High School the same year as the suspect, said he never would have suspected Geschwendt would commit six murders. "Here's a guy who looked like he wouldn't hurt a fly," he said. "He was a very wimpy-type person. You never know."

"It was a shock that he confessed to something like that," Dave Clee said. "It's a good thing those TV shows on now weren't on then—the ones where they say don't talk to anybody before you talk to your lawyer. If George had talked to a lawyer before he talked to anybody else, he might be out today."

Almost five decades later, Lieutenant Zajac was asked if he could have made a case against Geschwendt if he had the gun but no confession. "Probably," he said with a smile, "But getting the confession made it a lot easier."

CHAPTER 15

A Doleful Gasp

In a bizarre twist of fate, the surviving members of the Abt family were on their way to kill the Geschwendt family.

A couple days after the murders, news reporters had peppered Chief Michaels with questions about a rumored arrest. The chief promised they'd be the first to know when he made an arrest. He kept that promise. That is exactly the way it happened.

Chief Michaels told newspaper and TV reporters who the killer was before he told the two survivors.

When word that Larry Michaels was holding an early-morning press conference to announce an arrest hit our newsroom, editors scrambled to find three news reporters to cover it.

Although it was after midnight, I was assigned to go to the Abt house and ask Michael and Clifford's reaction to the news.

Two other reporters were assigned to attend the 12:30 a.m. press conference. The plan was for one of them to slip away as soon as he got the name of the suspect and phone me at the Abts' house with any details that might help me interview Michael and Clifford. There were no cell phones then, so I gave him the Abts' home number.

No one in the newsroom ever imagined Chief Michaels would tell reporters who they arrested before he told Michael and Clifford. It wasn't just a breach of courtesy; it was unsafe. The chief knew the Geschwendt home was directly across the street from the Abts', and the Abts kept guns in their house.

A reporter at the packed press conference overheard a patrol lieutenant tell another officer that he didn't see me in the crowd, and he hoped I wasn't at the Abt house spilling the news. I was at the house, but I definitely was not spilling the news.

When I arrived a little past midnight, several cars were parked in the Abts' driveway and the kitchen and living room were flushed with light. I was relieved they were up. I walked in with a notebook, ready to ask Michael and Clifford what they knew about the person under arrest. Suddenly, it seemed as if I were in an alternate dimension.

Michael and his friends were sitting around the teak coffee table that he and his father built. I noticed some guns in the center of the table and one across the back of the couch. A loaded shotgun was usually propped up against the front doorframe. They were talking and laughing. No one there seemed at all fazed by the arrest. Then it dawned on me that maybe they actually didn't know about it.

I walked into the kitchen, stunned. An instant later, I heard Clifford's robust voice ring out as he walked through the living room door, which became the preferred door after the slaughter in the kitchen. He sounded in great spirits.

Clifford's arrival made things worse. He was more mercurial than Michael. I calculated the news of the arrest would be out any minute. I wondered if the music I heard was coming from a radio station that might interrupt its broadcast for the announcement.

I didn't want the brothers who had been through so much to hear about their family's killer from a disembodied voice on the radio. Victims' families then didn't have the clout they have now, but, even then, announcing the suspect's name to the public before telling the survivors seemed nuts.

At that point, I just felt sadness for Clifford and Michael. I wasn't worried about violence at all, because I didn't know the murder suspect lived 112 feet away. Police had moved the Geschwendt family members to safety, but no one on the Abts' side of the street knew that yet.

The kitchen wall phone—the same one that deviled Geschwendt all day long on March 12—rang out sometime before 1 a.m. A friend of Michael's said it was for me. I took the receiver, propped my narrow reporter's notebook against the wall and began taking notes. Thankfully, everyone else was in the living room.

John Fisher, the reporter on the other end of the line, asked what was going on at the house. I told him that I couldn't figure it out. Everyone at the house acted as if they didn't know anything.

Fisher gave me the suspect's name—George Geschwendt. It didn't ring a bell. He didn't tell me Geschwendt lived across the street. I wrote GEORGE on my pad in precise block letters so I could read it later. There was a great deal of background noise wherever Fisher was. Trying to get the unusual last name down correctly, I asked him to spell it. Struggling to hear the correct spelling over the music and laughter coming from the living room, I repeated after him: G-E-S-C-H-W.

I was focusing on hearing Fisher's words over the music, not on what was going on around me. I thought I was alone in the kitchen. Just then, I sensed Edward "Beer Buddy" Myers, a pal of Michael, slowly passing behind me on his way to fetch a beer from the fridge. Buddy moved more slowly than most 20-year-olds, because he walked with a crutch. One of his legs had been amputated following a motorcycle collision. I shielded the notebook with my shoulder, but it was too late. Buddy had already glanced at the page where I had written GESCHWEN in clear block letters like kids do when they play hangman. By the time he made it across the kitchen, he had put the letters on my pad together in his head. He turned and shouted into the living room: "It's Geschwendt!" My shoulders froze in place.

"Geschwendt? What about him?" Michael yelled.

"It's Geschwendt!" Buddy bellowed, still in the kitchen but tottering toward the living room as fast as he could. "Geschwendt killed your family!"

The next sound that came from the living room was a heartbreaking, doleful gasp. Then, without a word, the two sons bolted for the door at the same instant. Their friends knotted behind them as they headed for the small Cape Cod across the street. Because I didn't know the suspect lived a front yard away, it made no sense at first. I thought they were going to pile into a car.

Michael and Clifford, both much too broad-shouldered to make it through the door at the same time, bounced backwards as their biceps slammed into the doorframe. They made it on the second try. Reporters from other outlets were arriving. They saw something entirely different from their perspective on the outside. They wrote that a fistfight had erupted between Michael and Clifford inside the house and they had battled through a doorway. Maybe there was a fistfight I couldn't see from the living room. Michael had a split lip the next morning.

In a bizarre twist of fate, the surviving members of the Abt family were on their way to kill the Geschwendt family.

The instant Michael and Clifford made their way onto the lawn, I realized they would be back any minute for the guns they'd forgotten in their haste. I looked over at the only other person left in the house, a friend of Michael's whom I had never met. At frightening moments, everyone's situational awareness surges. Without a word, both our eyes went to the guns. We promptly agreed we should hide them. The quickest place to do that was the dark basement where Michael and Clifford were least likely to look. Gambling that we'd have enough time, he quickly collected the guns around the living room. I knelt below the swinging basement doors and peered into the dark basement. The wooden steps had been removed as evidence, but I wanted to be certain glasses or gas cans hadn't taken their place. I couldn't see a thing. I did get a whiff of the rusty odor the seven blood spots still exuded.

When he handed me the armful of guns, I quickly rearranged them so all the barrels pointed away from the living room. Then I let them drop. They clanged as they hit the concrete. When it was done, I jumped to my feet and got out of the kitchen as fast as I could.

We each stood against a different sliver of the living room wall and caught our breath. I told him I was glad he knew how to handle the guns, because I didn't know whether they would go off when I dropped them. That was when he told me he didn't know either.

I noticed we both instinctively avoided the spot next to the piano where Geschwendt had stood. I flinched every time I walked past it and thought of him popping out like some macabre torsion-spring Jack in the Box. Surveying the room, I realized we missed one shotgun by the front door, but it was too late to do anything about that.

Suddenly, I realized some guns might be visible from the kitchen. I rushed back to look. As I was standing there peering into the pitch-black basement, I heard Clifford's voice erupt inside the living room. "Where are the guns?" he roared. "Where are the fucking guns?"

Before anyone could answer, his heavy footsteps were moving through the upstairs rooms. I wondered if he had taken two steps at a time.

Around the same time, the loaded shotgun that had been propped by the front door vanished. Michael was running barefoot across the front lawn wielding it like a stick to prevent his friends from restraining him before he made it across the pot-holed street to Geschwendt's. He was screaming, "I'll kill the whole family!"

Onlookers froze in the way people do when unanticipated events happen too fast. Suddenly, Officer Clee, who had been a standout on the Bensalem High football team 12 years earlier, darted after Michael, tackled him, and brought him down a few yards from Geschwendt's front door.

The Geschwendt house was so dark and deserted that the windows looked like black mirrors. The Abt house was anything but. Young men trickled in and out its front door. One of them flagged down a police officer and said, "You better do something. They have guns in there."

Detectives and uniformed police filed through looking for Michael and Clifford and guns. I didn't want Chief Michaels to spot me, so I rushed upstairs with Ed Allahand. Despite the 37-degree temperature, we opened a bedroom window so we could hear everything happening outside.

The black-and-white patrol cars arriving with their flashing red lights suddenly cast a magenta glow down Fleetwood Avenue. The Abts' friends drifted around the front yard. Some reporters were still arriving from the press conference. Watching the confusion outside from the second-story window was like watching a letterboxed action movie.

It was around 2 a.m., and I was still hoping to get out of the house undetected in time to report something. Mindful that the chief had threatened to arrest me a year earlier, I didn't want him to lay any of what happened that night on me. I wasn't the one who announced the suspect's name to the media before he told the survivors.

Shouts and curses rose from the living room for almost five minutes. Then we heard softer voices. Officers had corralled Clifford and Michael. From the pieces we could hear, it sounded as if they were gently reassuring them that Geschwendt was already in lockup and his family wasn't at home.

I wondered what the odds were for three boyhood friends raised in facing houses coming to this end. How could things have snowballed to the point where six innocent people were dead?

Then, from the upstairs window, I caught sight of a patrolman carrying guns from the house. I wondered if he had recovered the ones I had dropped into the basement or if he had discovered more in another room.

A few minutes later, I spotted John Sweeney, one of the reporters assigned to the press conference, walking back and forth in the street. He was assigned to report the action at the house and to file a story if the chief hassled me for being at the crime scene. The temperatures had dropped into the high twenties, but Sweeney was still outside when I headed for my car long after 2 a.m.

When we both returned to the newsroom, he bought me a hot tea from the vending machine in the cafeteria even though he was the one who spent the night out in the cold.

CHAPTER 16

The Morning After

The headline in the *Daily News* of Huntingdon, Pennsylvania, was "Murderer Found Across the Street." The *Tampa Bay Times* went with "'Strange Dude' is Charged with Six Pennsylvania Slayings." The *New York Daily News* head was a gross understatement: "The Bad Neighbor."

When Geschwendt's older brother, Fred, answered his front door the next morning, he found five detectives and a prosecutor looking back at him. One was armed with a search warrant.

His mother, Josephine Colon, took one glimpse at the warrant in Detective Ed Keyser's hands, broke into tears and dashed upstairs where she collapsed on a bed. Fred and the detectives followed her. Keyser read the search warrant aloud. Then detectives fanned out to hunt through her house and garage.

Led by Detective Edwards, the evidence technician, they took off with one pair of bluish-gray trousers, one pair of brown-checkered trousers, and some green socks. In the garage, they removed the black vinyl saddle bags from Geschwendt's Honda cycle. Lieutenant Zajac thought some castoff victim blood might have been transferred to the inside of the saddlebags from the items Geschwendt stashed there.

The police called an ambulance to take Mrs. Colon to Lower Bucks Hospital. They had no intention of arresting her or upsetting her. Detective Keyser was assigned to serve the warrant out of consideration for her. He was a familiar face because he had been to the house to pick up her son the previous evening.

Detectives Bob Eckert and Tom Scaricaciottoli were allowed to interview Mrs. Colon at the hospital, but, on her doctor's orders, a nurse was present during their visit. Physically upset and sobbing, Mrs. Colon said she just wanted to be alone with her children. This obviously was not the finale she imagined for her son who had earned a college degree.

Geschwendt's two older sisters declined to talk, too. They referred the detectives to an attorney.

On their way out of the hospital, Eckert and Scaricaciottoli spotted George's brother, the usually amiable Fred Geschwendt Jr. They asked him if he would speak to them. An older male told him not to talk.

***

Meanwhile, Fred's brother's high school yearbook photo was popping out of squat, black metal wirephoto machines in newspaper offices across the country. Before satellites and digital photos, newsrooms depended on noisy teletype machines to churn out wire service news stories the way player pianos churn out music. They clicked and clattered until all the news was typed onto floppy canary-yellow paper rolls so long that stories often coiled up on the floor. The photos that went with the news stories were transmitted to wirephoto machines over dedicated lines. It was like watching a very slow artist bring a picture to life.

I remember waiting for the *Courier Times*' wirephoto machine to print out the first photos of China during President Richard Nixon's historic trip there in 1972. Sandy Oppenheimer, the New Yorker who was executive editor at the *Courier Times*, walked out of the wire room waving a black-and-white photo of nondescript brick apartment buildings and shouted, "Red China looks like the Bronx." It did.

The wire machines were so noisy and threw off so much heat that most newspapers kept them in separate rooms. Editors working at their desks knew when a big story was on the way because loud bells sounded in the wire room. The Geschwendt arrest story set off bells.

It shuffled expectations, too. The boogeyman who menaced the township for 10 days was a bony, bespectacled community college graduate who blushed at the slightest embarrassment.

The "Good Evening" column in the *Courier Times* included this item: "Trevose, a pretty area with some of the finest people, is breathing a little easier tonight. The people there have been assured the six murders in the Abt home were a personal vendetta, and they have nothing to fear."

The headline in the *Daily News* in Huntingdon, Pennsylvania, was "Murderer Found Across the Street." The *Tampa Bay Times* went with "'Strange Dude' Charged with Six Pennsylvania Slayings." The *New York Daily News* head was a gross understatement: "The Bad Neighbor."

A teenage girl who had taken up a collection for the Abts recognized Geschwendt's photo on the front page of the newspaper. He donated 50 cents. She had no clue he was a spree killer when she knocked on his door, but she did remember him as peculiar. When she told him why she was collecting, he handed her a quarter, but he didn't say a word. She stood at the door for a moment, waiting for him to talk. He handed her another quarter and pulled the door shut.

A man who lived down Fleetwood Avenue said you could have knocked him over with a feather when he heard the news on the radio. He said the Geschwendts always kept their place pretty.

Margie Pekora, who lived one house away from Geschwendt, was unfazed when she thought the murders were the work of a professional hitman hired by a drug kingpin. Not so much when she heard of Geschwendt's arrest. Standing in front of the house, she told a reporter, "If I had known it was this family here, I would have been petrified."

"It kind of threw you off because you didn't expect it to be someone from the community," said Detective Eckert, who grew up there. "That was a really closeknit, idyllic kind of neighborhood. Everybody knew each other. People went to school together. They played ball together. It just wasn't something that happened in Trevose. It was like where the hell did that come from?"

Bob Hickey, one of the volunteer firemen who had pumped out the Abts' pool, was startled when he heard Geschwendt murdered a family because Clifford and Michael gave him attitude: "He picked them off like they were dogs. All this because they called you names?" Hickey said. "I got picked on for years—all through school. Anybody with a name like Hickey got ridiculed all the time. That he killed six people because of that really shook me. Life is precious."

Neighbors buzzed about the evils on the Abts' side of Fleetwood Avenue for 10 days, but no one suspected a problem on the other side of the street. Dave Clee said police would have suspected Geschwendt immediately if they knew his past, but they didn't.

Tino Colon, Geschwendt's stepfather, left the neighborhood in 1971, but he returned to express his condolences to Michael after the massacre. When they were face-to-face, Colon was overcome by emotion. All he could do was cry.

★★★

Bensalem Township detectives had made a solid arrest in a sextuple murder in 10 days, with heavyweight aid from the county and one very lucky break, but without benefit of DNA, computer databases, street cameras, genealogy databases, cell tower pings, facial recognition software or Google. It was a feat even 21st-century police departments can't always replicate.

The morning after the arrest, temperatures veered into the upper '60s, and Michael came out of the house barefoot with a beer can in one hand and a split lip left over from the previous night. His flannel shirt was open, and a silver cross hung around his neck. Reporters knotted around him.

He said he hadn't talked to Geschwendt in about two months, and neither he nor his brother had any real contact with him in eight or nine years. He added that he never would have suspected him.

Michael said the boys were all best friends when his family first moved to Trevose. They hung out together, built forts together and got in trouble together until middle school when Geschwendt's mother forbade him to play with the Abts. He said his first thought when he heard his old playmate killed his family was to blow George's head off, but he realized that was senseless because he was already jailed.

While reporters were circling Michael, one spotted Geschwendt's brother, Fred, standing yards away in front of his mother's house, a cigarette hanging out of his mouth as he tried to get his car started so he could leave the neighborhood. The 34-year-old said he didn't understand why his brother would want to kill the Abts. His mother, he said, had been admitted to the hospital where she was being treated for shock.

After police revealed how Geschwendt had squeezed himself in to the narrow space next to the piano, I realized I might need to know exactly how narrow it was when I covered his upcoming mass murder trial. I didn't want to whip out a measuring tape and reignite dark thoughts for Michael and Clifford, but I did want to know the measurement. I knew I'd need it for an accurate story later.

I stood against the wall by the thermostat trying not to be noticed as I lined my shoulder up with the doorframe. I could see the space between it and the piano was slightly more than one inch wider than my shoulders. That night, back at my cabin on the cliff, I used a yellow measuring tape to gauge that my shoulders were a tad over 15 inches, so the space was no wider than 17 inches.

After I did it, I shuddered at how peculiar what I was doing was. I thought measuring a serial killer's hiding spot was the ultimate one-off thing. Nonetheless, I added the measurement to my notebook.

Then I went to sleep in my cabin that seemed so safe and remote but was actually fewer than two miles from the killer's hiding spot. Later, I learned the picturesque cabin just across the cliff from mine had been rented as a meth lab.

***

George Geschwendt was reunited with Lieutenant Zajac and Detective Batezel that morning. They transported him from the Bristol Township Police Station to Bucks County Prison in Doylestown, usually about a 40-minute trip, but they planned a side trek to Washington Crossing State Park on the Delaware River. They hoped Geschwendt would point out the exact spot where he ditched his rubber-soled Sears boots, the ones that matched the bloody footprint in the Abt basement and the dusty one in the Vogenbergers' attic.

They pulled into a McDonald's on the way, and Batezel walked inside to get a burger, fries, and a large Coke for Geschwendt. While Zajac and his prisoner were waiting in the car, Geschwendt suddenly blurted out that, when he was sitting alone in the cell the night before, he started thinking about spending the rest of his life in jail.

Zajac listened.

Geschwendt griped that he could hear the Bristol Township police officers joking about him when they thought he couldn't hear them. He grumbled that everything he did to improve his life didn't help.

He joined the Navy. He earned an associate degree. He went to truck driving school. No matter what he tried, he still couldn't get a job. He either lacked experience, or he was overqualified. He was always starting over.

And now, newspapers were reporting that he was a bachelor who lived at home with his mother, a loner who never left the house.

He was correct. Even readers in Miami knew he had never dated a woman.

The 10-mile detour to Washington's Crossing was a washout for the detectives. Geschwendt led them to the spot along the riverbank where he believed he tossed his boots and gloves, but they found zilch. They even tossed another boot into the water, hoping to follow its trajectory to the originals, but the swift current simply carried it out of sight.

When Geschwendt arrived at the county prison later that day, he was assigned a cell in the maximum-security red-lock section for his own protection. Red-lock prisoners leave their cells only two hours a day for exercise. Guards took it one step further for Geschwendt. His two hours were slated at night, when prison activity was at its lowest ebb.

In Trevose, after 10 days of speculation about drug activity at the Abt house, Chief Michaels held a press conference to announce the murders were not drug related in any way. They were grudge killings. Suddenly, as if someone flipped a switch, Clifford Abt was in the clear.

That was a relief for him. The anonymity of evil had kept Clifford up at night while he was in jail. He lay awake hour after hour in his cell, thinking who he did business with who would have murdered his parents, brother and sisters. He was stumped. He went over it and over it, eliminating suspects in his mind. It was a lot for a 23-year-old who still lived with his parents.

Suddenly, after the arrest, there was a context switch. Evil, apparently, lived on the opposite side of the street. Clifford was officially a victim of George Geschwendt, just like the rest of his family. The accepted narrative kept morphing the way reflections in a fun house mirror shift.

When I interviewed Clifford about the sudden turnabout after he was released from custody, he was still smarting from the way he was treated after his family's deaths. "I'd like to thank all these people—lines and lines of them—who came down to the police station with information about me. I saw them come to the police station window, people I didn't even know," he said. "I never saw them before, and they knew all these things about me. I especially appreciate all the know-it-alls who know more than I do about myself. Please ask them to stop around and tell me what my life is all about. Maybe they can start eating their words with salt and pepper."

Even when he was a kid, people tended to suspect Clifford. Josephine Colon thought he was a bad influence on her son, George Geschwendt, who turned out to be a mass murderer.

Clifford's eyes teared up when he told me how grateful he was for the kindnesses Bensalem police showed him. He said he would always be grateful to his fiancée's family for helping him get out of jail. He saved his rancor for his aunts and uncles and grandmothers who huddled around his parents' caskets before they were lowered into the ground and left him standing in the back of the crowd with only his fiancée and his attorney to comfort him. He said that galled him.

He said he was more broken up on the inside than on the outside. In his head, he was still imagining what his parents, his little brother and his sisters went through.

While Clifford remained distant from his extended family, he and Michael slowly grew closer for a while after the arrest. Clifford said he was glad Michael was officially no longer a suspect. "My brother's all I've got left," he said. Michael told reporters they had become "pretty damn close" since Clifford moved into the house, but they still had riffs.

That spring, though, things were looking up. They had their home back. The likely killer was in custody. Insurance papers were filed. And just beyond the front porch, crocuses, one of the first flowers of spring, were in full bloom. It could have been a new beginning—but a sextuple murder trial loomed ahead.

The Abt brothers' giving some lip to Geschwendt was the closest thing to a motive that police could find for the murder of six innocent people.

Lucy Edwards, whose husband Bill worked the case, remembered him saying some of the Abt kids called Geschwendt "banana nose" on the school bus.

John Gottschalk recalls coming to Geschwendt's aid two or three times in the early '70s. The much bigger Clifford was whacking Geschwendt in the back of the head repeatedly as he walked right behind him and called him "faggot." "I was the bigger guy, so I told the Abt brothers to leave him alone or I was going to rip their behinds," Gottschalk said. "They were tall, and George was shorter, and they picked on the easier victim. They singled him out. He didn't come from the best family. His father wasn't in the picture. I was brought up with a religious background. It just hurt me to see what they did."

Geschwendt didn't mention physical abuse in his confession, only name-calling, so police took it in the context of the '70s attitudes toward bullying. "Kids, boys more so, were taught to deal with it," Detective Eckert said. "It was part of growing up. Sticks and stones will break my bones, but names will never hurt me was the saying kids were taught. Verbal bullying never justified an aggressive response. You were to just shake it off and move on. Having good comebacks was always admired."

Rich Fink, Geschwendt's attorney, didn't underscore the bullying in the courtroom. "I never really believed in the bullying, except maybe some minor amounts," Fink said. "It was less than helpful to go into it, since it could never justify this amount of killing."

Fink said the lesson for today from the Abt murders is that time bombs do surround us and they must be spotted by teachers, friends, neighbors and psychologists so they can be defused.

Michael denied harassing Geschwendt. Clifford said he had not paid any attention to Geschwendt at all since his mother had stopped him from playing with them when they were in middle school. Other friends said Geschwendt was harassed, but no amount of bullying could justify six murders.

On March 24, the front-page "Good Morning" column in the *Courier Times* included this short item on motive: "The Abt sons can't find a motive for this suspect, but can anyone who can shoot six people in cold blood be sane?"

Geschwendt hadn't only murdered five of the Abts and Margie's boyfriend. He had also upended Michael's and Clifford's futures. Dozens of family moments were automatically wiped from their calendars for decades ahead—birthdays, graduations, Mother's Days, weddings, baptisms, fishing trips.

As news photographers' flashbulbs popped around them, Michael and Clifford were left adrift with no other immediate family and no jobs.

Clifford told reporters he had some experience doing mechanical work, but he'd work at anything. He said if he didn't know anything about the job, he'd work for free and start taking a salary once he learned.

Suddenly, Clifford and Michael had to fend for themselves. They had to take on all the responsibilities of homeowners, including the county tax bill that landed in their mailbox the morning after the murders.

In a matter of weeks, neighbors would once again be grumbling about unwelcome activity at the Abt house.

CHAPTER 17

One Big Unhappy Story

> Hundreds of people crisscrossed the grounds and roamed through the 10-room murder scene eating hot dogs and drinking Cokes from a makeshift concession stand set up aside the murdered couple's barn. Playing in the background was the constant trill of the auctioneer.

After Geschwendt's arrest, gossip about him came flowing into the Bensalem police station the same way gossip about Clifford Abt had just a week earlier. Henry Maronski, who had told police he didn't see anything out of the ordinary one week earlier, realized something that seemed ordinary to him then might be important to them now. The day after the murders, he saw the usually tight-lipped Geschwendt walking up and down Fleetwood Avenue chatting amiably with the lookie-loos milling around the Abt house. He was hiding in plain sight. Maronski said he saw him talking with two news reporters.

Police spent almost five months cementing their case against Geschwendt. They reinterviewed witnesses. They awaited lab reports. They checked every detail of his lengthy confession.

Sergeant Berry was dispatched to a thick woods to find the light-colored abandoned truck Geschwendt said he used for target practice. He found fresh holes the size of a .22-caliber bullet, but those holes were surrounded with hundreds of older, rust-encircled ones. He noticed a second vehicle stippled with more rusty holes. The sergeant had happened upon an ersatz neighborhood firing range.

On March 29, Clifford received the letter his mother wrote to him the night before she was murdered. She had addressed it to him at Bucks

County Prison, but it missed him when he moved to the Bensalem holding cell. No one recognized its importance until Clifford's attorney retrieved it 17 days after Peggy mailed it.

On March 30, a U-Haul moving van pulled up to the Geschwendt house. A police escort waited while two men loaded furniture into the van.

On April 1, Geschwendt's preliminary hearing drew a crowd to a district court wedged between a hoagie shop and a dog obedience school in a strip shopping center. Rich Fink represented Geschwendt. Every person who entered the 27-seat courtroom was frisked because there were credible threats to Geschwendt's life—and Fink's.

Inside the small courtroom, the Abt brothers chatted amiably, in sharp contrast to the way they distanced themselves from one another at their parents' funeral 19 days earlier. They huddled with police officers and took a smoke break together. Sitting side-by-side in the front row, they turned to watch two Bensalem officers usher their old playmate to his seat.

Geschwendt's stringy light-brown hair grazed the collar of his green dress shirt. He wore metal-rimmed glasses that partially obscured his thick eyebrows. A narrow brush mustache topped his thin upper lip. His brown eyes darted around at the capacity crowd as he walked to his seat, but he sat still and silent once the hearing began. The officers who escorted Geschwendt told reporters they tried to include him in their conversations, but he rarely said anything. When he did, his affect was flat.

Geschwendt didn't chit-chat with his attorney, Rich Fink, either. He didn't even make eye contact. His eyes darted around when he talked, but they rarely locked on the person he was answering.

When they discussed his case, Geschwendt made no small talk. He never laughed. He never cried. He was emotionless. "He wasn't one of those clients where you feel you can put your hand on his shoulder," Fink said.

The only reason they would talk was if Fink needed some information from him. It was as if Geschwendt were still following the speech pattern he learned at home, where the only conversation was a yes or no answer to his father's questions.

When an attorney is going for an insanity defense, he doesn't really want a defendant who noticeably takes part in his own defense in front of the jurors, but Geschwendt made no effort at all to help his attorney save his life.

The hearing was over in five minutes. As soon as the first murder charge for Mrs. Abt's death was read, Fink stood. He told the magistrate there was no point in reading further. His client would waive his right to a preliminary hearing on all six murder charges. The Abt brothers were quickly ushered from the tightly packed courtroom before Geschwendt was led out.

Although it did not make the national news the way Geschwendt's preliminary hearing did, on the same day on the other side of the country, three computer hobbyists started their own company. Steve Jobs and Steve Wozniak and Ronald Wayne formed the Apple Computer Company. They hoped to sell small computers that people could use right in their homes.

★★★

Bensalem Police sought advice from the DA's office every step of the way because Zajac was exacting. He didn't want to chance anything going awry at the trial in the modernistic Bucks County Courthouse in Doylestown.

The sleek 14-year-old court building, which occupies the highest bluff in the historic borough, was controversial. Many residents believed the mammoth brick and precast-concrete courthouse was out of place on a block of stately law offices and charming 19th-century homes. Its detractors called it "the toilet."

The mid-century-modern structure got its nickname because pilots said its five-story rotunda combined with its seven-story rectangular office building looked like a giant toilet from the air.

Geschwendt moved robotically as he was led into the courthouse for his arraignment on April 28, handcuffed and flanked by two sheriffs who looked like extras from a caper movie in their fedoras, dark glasses, suit coats and busy ties.

When the lawmen stepped away, court watchers saw Geschwendt inch forward wearing the same open-necked green shirt and black pants he wore to his preliminary hearing. Several whispered among themselves. One speculated the suspect was wearing the same clothes to bolster an insanity defense, and he said it loud enough for everyone in the rows around him to hear. Later, Fink told reporters his client was simply wearing the clothes he had.

Geschwendt stood stiffly and silently for most of the session. He entered a not guilty plea. When he answered the judge's questions, his responses were less formal than most defendants', almost flippant. When the judge asked him if he understood the legal motion, he said, "Yeah. I heard it." When he was asked if he were willing to wait two months to come to trial, he shrugged his bony shoulders and said, "It's okay with me."

That gave listeners a rare chance to hear a snippet of the voice that embarrassed Geschwendt. It wasn't shrill or soprano. It was deep.

His trial date was set for July 12, exactly four months after the slaughter. It was scheduled in Courtroom Five, the largest one in the building, the same one that was jam-packed for the sensational Mary Mamon murder trial seven years earlier.

★★★

Geschwendt told a defense psychiatrist the mass murder was his only achievement in life. That irked Patrolman Dave Clee, whose quick-thinking kept Michael Abt from discovering his family's disfigured bodies. "Geschwendt didn't achieve anything," Clee said. "He was an unsuccessful killer. He didn't kill the ones he wanted to kill. He killed Kathy and little Johnny. They never did shit to him, and Mr. and Mrs. Abt and Garson Engle never did anything to him. He got the wrong people."

While Geschwendt was awaiting trial, a new family bought the small Cape Cod where he grew up. His mother and brother had moved out at the end of March. By late May, the Abt brothers would have new across-the-street neighbors. One of their friends joked that the newcomers had to be better.

★★★

On May 27, four miles away in Langhorne Borough, a young man tried to maneuver a washing machine out the back door of the brick farmhouse where the Vogenbergers had been murdered 11 weeks earlier. The executors of the Vogenbergers' estate had hired an auctioneer to sell the couples' personal belongings and farm equipment. Boxes filled with the their books and canning jars and old waffle irons dotted the lawn. Heavy, old-fashioned bureaus rested on the grass.

By 10 a.m. on the morning of the auction, parked cars and pickup trucks lined the curbs around the farm. Nearly 1,000 bargain hunters and curiosity seekers turned out, a number the auctioneer said was about double the average house sale, according to *Courier Times* reporter Bill Newill. Plainclothes policemen were rumored to be among the crowd.

Hundreds of people crisscrossed the grounds and roamed through the 10-room murder scene eating hot dogs and drinking Cokes from a makeshift concession stand set up aside the murdered couple's barn. Playing in the background was the constant trill of the auctioneer who segued from the current price of an item to the asking price and back again, with a few nonsense words interspersed.

A man carried off a portrait of a Vogenberger ancestor who died in the 1918 flu pandemic, possibly for its large antique gilded frame. A homemade Monopoly game went for $5. A man paid $4 for salvage rights to whatever was left in Ed Vogenberger's workshop. Ed's old Ford tractor was the hot item. It sold for $3,750.

After his brother's yard was nearly emptied, Ralph Vogenberger, a large man in a brown leisure suit, summed it all up. In the Carolina drawl he acquired in the 51 years since he left Bucks County, he said, "It's certainly been a big, unhappy story, hasn't it?"

CHAPTER 18

You Killed a Saint Bernard

> Rich Fink, Geschwendt's lawyer, had already warned him at the outset that his case was nearly impossible to win, because, in addition to killing six humans of all ages, he had killed a Saint Bernard, and she was named Heidi.

In Doylestown, the county seat, legal offices were abuzz about the Geschwendt case to be tried there in six weeks.

Judge Paul R. Beckert, a 55-year-old no-nonsense Republican with a booming voice, would preside. A former district attorney, he was generally considered the second-toughest judge on the county bench. The line on him from convicts was, he didn't discriminate against anyone; he was tough on everyone.

First in his law class at Villanova, he was generally considered fair and knowledgeable, although sometimes rigid. Outside the courtroom he was known as "The Duke," a handle he acquired as a kid. The name stuck because it fit a judge who imposed strict rules in his courtroom, including one that barred female lawyers from wearing pantsuits when arguing before him.

Beckert's son said he looked like a judge, he sounded like a judge, and, if he hadn't become a judge, he could have played one on TV.

The judge helmed the Mary Mamon hammer murder case in 1969, the most sensational murder trial in Bucks County history until the Geschwendt case. Now he would preside over the Geschwendt case, too.

Ken Biehn, the 37-year-old district attorney, took the high-profile Geschwendt case. As a star high school athlete and one of the youngest DAs in county history, the Duke Law graduate was accustomed to success. The statewide Jaycees had recently honored him as one of the 10 outstanding young men in Pennsylvania.

Rich Fink, the public defender, was only four years out of Temple Law, but, within a year, he would be running the county public defender's office. This son of a conservative local attorney drove a yellow Porsche convertible and had a paneled office waiting for him at his father's Levittown firm if he wanted it. Instead, he chose to defend the clients nobody else wanted. As a 28-year-old from a privileged background, Fink was moved by the parents who put on their best clothes and shined their shoes to come to the public defender's office because they had never spoken with a lawyer before.

Both sides put countless hours in on the Geschwendt case.

Biehn, the DA, and his assistant, Dave Heckler, spent hundreds of hours on the case. Maryann Costello, their secretary, often worked into the night typing reports.

The DA, who majored in psychology in college, read dozens of books on insanity defenses because he knew Fink was searching for a top psychiatrist who would interview Geschwendt and testify he was a paranoid schizophrenic. One book told the story of infamous Philadelphia killer Joseph Kallinger, who had been diagnosed as paranoid schizophrenic. Although he later tried to swallow a spoon and he lit himself on fire while trying to fry an egg on his head, Kallinger was convicted and sentenced to two life terms. Biehn was hoping for a similar outcome for his case.

Rich Fink, Geschwendt's public defender, worked such long hours on his cases that his first marriage fell apart. When he had a case, his client was number one in his life for as long as it took. He would eat, sleep and prepare his defense.

He and co-counsel Terry Clemmons worked into the nights. They knew they were all that stood between Geschwendt and the electric chair. They knew the confession Zajac and Batezel extracted from their client wouldn't help. Nor would what Geschwendt told Detective Batezel—that if he ever got free, he would kill Michael and Clifford.

"What he actually said was, 'If I ever get out, I'll finish the job,'" Fink said. "That's pretty devastating to your case because it's a good, good, good reason to kill him. That was the worst piece of evidence in the trial."

Fink had already warned Geschwendt at the outset that his case was nearly impossible to win, because, in addition to killing six humans of all ages, he had killed a Saint Bernard, and she was named Heidi. "I told him: 'You killed a Saint Bernard. There's no way to win a case when you kill a Saint Bernard,'" Fink said. "He understood."

Fink was known around the courthouse as an attorney who never lost his sense of humor despite the long odds given to most of his clients. Although lie detector tests rarely ended well for his clients, he admired the talents of expert polygraph examiners. He bought one examiner a joke gift from a religious supply store. It was a small bronze door plaque with the words, "Confessions Taken Daily 10 a.m. to 3 p.m."

Fink's practical jokes were legendary around the courthouse. In the days before DNA, he once petitioned a prosecutor to supply semen from a man involved in a case so he could have blood typing done. While the defense and the prosecution were arguing the point in court, Fink convinced a pal in the prosecutor's office to put some white glue in an open paper cup and deliver it to Fink's secretary to freak her out.

He once sneaked into another attorney's office and slipped the mouthpiece out of his phone. He knew it worked when he heard the other attorney screaming on the other side of the wall, "Are you deaf? What the fuck is wrong with you? Goddamnit, I asked you a question!" When the attorney realized someone had removed his mouthpiece, he burst into the public defender's office and ripped a phone off the wall. But not Fink's phone. It was his office mate's. He got the wrong guy.

Fink and Clemmons would occasionally take a few minutes to let off steam with the other public defenders before leaving for the night. They played "Mickey Mouse ball," a game they made up using a volleyball with the Disney mouse printed on the side. Remaining seated in their wheeled desk chairs, they'd roll back and forth across the floor of their office, which was located directly above the county commissioners' suite. Players had to keep the ball in the air even if they had to dive for it, sending their chairs careening across the room or crashing to the floor in loud thuds. One of the commissioners buttonholed Fink one day, and asked, "What do you guys do at night up there?"

Sometimes, while they waited for a night verdict, they'd have a beer in the office. Once, the presiding judge dropped in for a drink before the verdict came in.

By 1976, Fink had come a long way from one of his early cases when one client was so sure he was going to jail that he handed Fink his wallet and his car keys as the jurors filed back into their seats. It wasn't necessary; he was acquitted.

Fink was winning cases, but this was his first murder case, and there were six human victims and a dog named Heidi. That would be a tall order for any defense attorney.

Fink placed an urgent call to the Geschwendts asking them all to share any facts about George's home life that might help humanize him to the jurors. His mother and sister came to Fink's office.

Betty Kennedy screwed up the courage to reveal some of the worst scenes from her brother's childhood. His mother just sat close-mouthed across the table. Fink, who was working day and night to keep her son out of the electric chair, pleaded with her, but she just sat there, almost catatonic. She gave him zip.

Frustrated, he shouted that the state wanted to electrocute her son. His exact words were "to boil his brain until it came out his ears." It didn't seem to register.

Fink became so frustrated that he threw a pen at her chest. Snapping out of her stupor, she screamed that she was going right downstairs to file a complaint about him at the office of the district attorney, the man who was hoping to execute her son.

Because Fink was suddenly in the spotlight as the twenty-something who would run point on the biggest murder case in county history, he was getting unsolicited but welcome advice from experienced news reporters. Marty Van Atta, a freelance reporter for the *Philadelphia Inquirer*, and Pat Wandling, who had worked in radio and newspapers, correctly guessed Fink was not ready for the international publicity the case would generate. They gave him some heads-ups on handling the reporters who would soon be coming his way. It was practical advice on how reporters work. One simple tip: attorneys are not really expected to comment if a reporter calls them at home late at night and asks them to respond to something a detective or prosecutor just said.

Even if they handled the media flawlessly, Fink and Clemmons faced potent evidence from Bensalem police and an all-in prosecution team. As Deputy DA Alan Rubenstein put it, "This is not the type of case where you exert half-hearted efforts. It is the willful destruction of an entire family."

***

Meanwhile, the Vogenberger double murder case was growing cold. Langhorne residents celebrated the centennial of their town's renaming without Ed and Marguerite, longtime members of the Historic Langhorne Association. The festivities drew thousands to the borough on a sunny day in June. Townspeople buried a time capsule. A parade of marchers and vehicles coiled around the downtown blocks for 90 minutes.

That same day, another group of about 75 gathered beneath the tall trees behind the Vogenberger farmhouse. They listened to a professional auctioneer selling Ed Vogenberger's childhood home and the 14 acres of prime land that surrounded it. Farmers, land speculators and the curious turned out for the auction. Relatives of the murder victims wanted to sell the place because it had been vacant since March when the couple was murdered.

The opening price for the house, the outbuildings and the farmland was $25,000, but at least six bidders jumped in. Within 10 minutes the farm was sold for more than three times that. A Bensalem farmer snatched it for $88,000.

Neighbors who came out of curiosity were surprised the prime property sold for so little.

After the agreement of sale was signed, Ed Vogenberger's genial brother Ralph shook the buyer's hand and said, "Good luck. I hope you enjoy it as much as I did when I was growing up here."

CHAPTER 19

The Trial Begins

As they were prepping for the trial, defense attorney Rich Fink asked the psychiatrists if Geschwendt could be cured. They both laughed. "What's funny about that?" Fink asked. "He would need decades of close, personal, intense psychotherapy, and I wouldn't want to be his therapist," one said. Then they both laughed again. "What's funny about that?" Fink asked again. "He will want to kill whoever gets close to him," one of them said.

Jury selection for the Geschwendt trial began July 12, a warm, cloudless day in Bucks County. If the murders had not happened, Margie Abt would have been enjoying her first day of vacation. The week of July 12 was one of the two weeks she had reserved at the beginning of the year.

Minutes after the first group of potential jurors filed into the courtroom, it became clear that some of them wanted to take a hard pass. One man was an expectant father. One husband insisted he had to return home each night to give his wife her spending money. The treasurer of a credit union said serving on a jury would set things back at his office like you wouldn't believe.

One man insisted he would require an exceptionally hard mattress with a sheet of plywood under it. One man warned he took five pills a day, and one was a water pill. A woman said no one would look after her electrical appliances if she were on jury duty. She said her refrigerator might need defrosting.

Edward Cann, a steelworker, said he would trust a police officer more than any other witness. He said that was just the way he was raised. He was excused.

A woman said she couldn't judge fairly because the sextuple murder with children involved was such a "horrendous crime." She was excused, too.

A man brought up as a Quaker said he had not determined in his own mind whether or not he could vote for the death penalty. He was also excused.

The judge excused a man who worked with Jack Abt, a man whose father was dying of cancer, and a woman who couldn't hear the question, "Do you have any kind of hearing impairment at all?"

Fink and Biehn went through all 78 potential jurors without finding a dozen who were acceptable to both sides and willing to be sequestered at a local Holiday Inn for two weeks.

In an unusual step, the judge used an old statute Fink discovered to authorize the county sheriff to pull in unsuspecting passersby right off the street and press them into jury duty on the spot.

Fink said he had found the statute because he always made it a point to research until he knew more than anyone else about any point of law that might help his case. He wasn't bragging. He learned to do that early on in his career after he made the mistake of asking a senior attorney what the law was in a particular situation. The older lawyer answered him: "Are you a fucking lawyer? Do you know where the law library is?"

Geschwendt showed no interest in any of the jurors who would decide whether he lived or died. He sat at the defense table doodling science-fiction creatures and sipping water from a paper cup.

Not one member of his own family came to support him, but the two Abts he left alive sat together in the front row of the spectator gallery, a few feet from his own seat.

***

Fink had limited experience but keen instincts. When he spotted a potential juror thumbing through a dog-breeding magazine in the jury assembly room, he knew he had a problem.

When the dog lover took the stand, Fink, with well-built questions, got her to admit she really couldn't be fair to someone who would kill a dog. She was excused.

***

When he noticed one prospective juror kept smiling at the district attorney, Fink asked him if he knew Biehn. The juror said he'd known Biehn since they played basketball together in high school. Biehn was an indispensable six-foot-four-inch forward on the Quakertown High School team in the late '50s. The DA, the affable son of a prominent Bucks County attorney, was known campaigning door-to-door and knowing many of his constituents personally.

***

Fink recalled one man from the jury pool was wearing cufflinks. Fink's first impression was that the man was dressed much more formally than most of the jury pool. He said he didn't like people dressing up conservatively to do their duty to the court and put their neighbors away, so he instantly disliked him. When he took a closer look, he noticed something peculiar.

The man's cufflinks were shaped like miniature silver handcuffs. The potential juror had already testified he could be fair and base his decision on the facts of the case, so Fink complimented him on his cufflinks and casually asked, "Where'd you get those?"

Biehn at once objected, Fink said.

The judge instructed the man to answer the question.

"I got them here," the man said.

"Who did you get them from?" Fink asked.

Fink said Biehn objected again.

The judge overruled him again.

"From the prosecutor," the man said.

"Which prosecutor?" Fink asked.

Biehn objected again, but the judge was curious too.

"That one," the man said, pointing to Biehn.

Judge Beckert asked the man if he could obey the law and presume the defendant is not guilty. He said he could.

Fink, who didn't buy it, quizzed the man with a litany of long-winded questions geared to educate the other juror candidates on presumption of innocence. After 30 minutes of it, the judge seemed to realize Fink could go on forever. He excused the man with the handcuff cufflinks.

★★★

Five men and seven women were sworn in to decide Geschwendt's fate—a clerk, a typist, a homemaker, a steelworker, an accountant, a bank teller, a store manager, a retired engineer, a nursing student, a retired government employee, a practical nurse and a company vice president. The alternate jurors were both female—a secretary and a church musician.

Fink managed to get all the dog lovers off the jury, but none of 14 individuals who would decide Geschwendt's fate had any problem with the death penalty.

★★★

The 12 jurors and two alternates stayed at the Holiday Inn in trendy New Hope, Pennsylvania, 11 miles from the courthouse. They ate their meals isolated from the other motel guests. They could listen to radio or television only in the supervised juror recreation area. They were allowed no mail or phone calls. They could order alcohol on nights when the court was not in session, but only if they paid their own bar bills and did all their drinking in the jurors' dining room.

★★★

As the trial date approached, the judge nixed Fink's request for metal detectors to screen spectators, even though Geschwendt, Fink and

Clemmons had all received credible death threats. One came from Clifford Abt. He spotted a court official at a gas station, drove up to him, leaned out the widow and said, "That man in your jail isn't going to stay alive long enough to stand trial."

Clifford, probably still reeling from his loved ones' murders, seesawed over what he wished for their killer. Once, during a brief interview in the room where his parents were killed, he first said he didn't want to take revenge on Geschwendt himself, but did want to see him die in the electric chair. Then, two minutes later, he told me he had already made "arrangements" for Geschwendt at the county prison. "He might as well print condolence cards ahead of time," he said, "because he's already dead."

★★★

The Abt case was still in the headlines from New York City to Billings, Montana, as the trial opened on July 12. Seats in the courtroom filled in nothing flat. Women in cork-bottomed shoes and men sporting permed hair and muttonchop sideburns stayed lined up outside the courtroom's oversized wooden doors even after court was already in session, hoping some court-watchers might relinquish their seats when they needed the restroom.

One man posed as a reporter to get one of the reserved seats in the press section, but he was quickly found out.

A couple who managed to wrangle two seats mentioned that they had also attended every session of the Mary Mamon trial.

Heads swiveled as Geschwendt emerged from inside the trio of deputies who circled him as he entered the sleek, wood-accented courtroom on the first day of testimony. Two women bent forward in their seats to get a better look at him. One of them whispered to the other that he was wearing the same open-necked green shirt and wrinkled black pants he wore to his preliminary hearing and his arraignment.

One reporter said Geschwendt looked like he had dead eyes, but he didn't. His eyes were the only moving part in his otherwise expressionless face. He seemed to be taking it all in, and maybe even enjoying the attention.

With all the focus on Geschwendt, few people in the courtroom realized that Rich Fink, his young public defender, had never presented a murder case before. It didn't help Fink's nerves that several seats in the front were reserved for older, more experienced attorneys who might drop in to watch him spar with Biehn.

The Abt sons' friends, who sat as close to Geschwendt as they could get, rattled Fink. Some made low, buzzing noises to mimic the sound they thought an electric chair would make. The judge couldn't hear them from the bench, but Fink could.

The largest section in the courtroom was reserved for members of the press. Many of us had covered the case since the beginning—watching from the street as Heidi's carcass was carried to the truck, standing elbow-to-elbow in the cramped police station lobby waiting for news, and saddened but still scribbling as 30 pallbearers rolled casket after casket up the long center aisle at Saint Dominic's. Now we were sitting in the courtroom scanning certain faces for reactions that we would add to our stories like chefs add carrots to their soups.

At the break, one reporter asked why Geschwendt never seemed to have more than two or three men guarding him. A deputy explained the goal was to draw as little attention as possible to Geschwendt. He said more deputies would be assigned if necessary. By the next week, there were five.

The courtroom was hushed as the district attorney and the defense attorney delivered their opening statements, but, while most sat in rapt attention, Geschwendt yawned, slouched, and doodled on a legal pad. He unwrapped the candy mints attorneys sometimes supply to mask their clients' prison breath. He lobbed them into his mouth repeatedly, leaving a hill of spent wrappers on his side of the defense table.

In a soft voice, Ken Biehn told the jurors a fast-paced story about Geschwendt breaking into the Abts' kitchen minutes after Michael walked out. He described how the defendant shot four innocent adults and two children in the face at close range and dragged their bodies to the basement.

When he said Mrs. Abt was shot in the face with such force that she fell backwards through the swinging doors and down the basement stairs, Clifford sat silently in the front row, grinding his teeth. He stared at the floor as Biehn described his mother's horrific last moments.

The district attorney promised to show that Geschwendt was legally sane when he slew six people. He said he would prove the killer planned every step of the mass homicide, even reporting his gun stolen in case it was ever traced back to him.

He sketched Geschwendt as a cool, calm and collected college graduate who was fully aware and frighteningly efficient when he set out to pick off the members of the Abt family one by one. Geschwendt didn't think he was smashing a beetle when he shot six people, Biehn said.

Fink stunned the courtroom when he admitted Geschwendt killed the Abts. He told the jurors he would prove his client he was not legally responsible for the shootings because he suffered from late-stage paranoid schizophrenia when he did it. Geschwendt was born amok, Fink said, and his bizarre family life aggravated the disease he had since birth.

Geschwendt didn't flinch when Fink told the jurors he would ask them to return a verdict of not guilty by reason of insanity. He displayed no reaction at all.

To convince the jurors that Geschwendt was preloaded with a mental disease at birth and his family life made it worse, Fink sketched young George's world. It was ruled by a brutal alcoholic who had less regard for his children than most people have for their pets, he said. The family members never touched each other and hardly even spoke to each other.

Judge Beckert interrupted Fink repeatedly, telling him to use his opening statement to show what he was going to prove. Fink, already nervous with more experienced attorneys watching from their reserved seats, had no other opening to give. So he pressed on.

"The fence around George's house describes his life," he told the jurors. He explained that Geschwendt's father's idea of a backyard fence was a tall wall of black railroad ties topped with barbed wire. His son called it his concentration camp.

As Fink pressed on, he noticed Judge Beckert starting to rise in his seat at one point and he saw the DA raise both his hands at another. He winced, but he kept talking.

He told the jurors the one exception in George Geschwendt's dire life was the lively, friendly, fun-loving Abt family across the street. He said Geschwendt became obsessed with them. He believed he was "elected" to kill them all. "He was totally out of touch with reality," Fink said.

"There was no motive here. There's only one reason, and it's sickness," Fink said. "Only a mentally ill person would kill the only family who ever befriended him."

"What happened on March 12 is a horrible thing," Fink said. "It's horrible beyond belief. We intend to prove to you the horror in this case runs much deeper than the things the district attorney has just outlined to you."

Fink sat down, relieved that he was able to deliver his opening because he had no Plan B.

"I got away with continuing to try to obtain some iota of sympathy for a mass murderer who had wiped out an entire family and brought terror to the vicinage," he said decades later. "But the judge remembered forever that I had disobeyed him continuously. If he had ever liked me, even a little, and he never had even that much liking for anyone at all, my usurpation of his authority was the end of that forever."

Fink had burned a big bridge with the judge. The prosecutor, on the other hand, would become a county judge himself within three years, and, when he did, Judge Beckert, a fellow Republican, would preside over his swearing in.

Detectives provided Ken Biehn with plenty of evidence, but he knew the order in which he unpacked it mattered. His plan was to present a parade of riveting prosecution witnesses with no delay in between so there was no time for doubts to surface in the jurors' minds. It would be well-ordered and lightning fast. He would sew it all together in his closing statement.

Witnesses testified Geschwendt bought a gun on March 5 and reported it stolen just 90 minutes later, the first step to proving he planned the massacre to the last detail. A Levittown gun dealer said he sold Geschwendt a .22-caliber revolver on March 5. Jules Scheidecker said Geschwendt also asked for an interchangeable magnum cylinder used to fire more deadly magnum bullets.

Michael Abt connected with the jury when he took the stand to describe coming home to a dark kitchen on the murder night. The jurors sat transfixed when Michael, in a soft voice, said he switched on the light and saw blood smeared on the kitchen floor and soaked into the living room rug. Choking back tears, the 22-year-old described finding his younger brother Johnny's blood-soaked sweatshirt near the family piano. His voice cracked as he said, "It looked like quite a bit of blood."

When photographers tailed Michael through the courthouse corridors at the next break, he warned them not to take his picture. "What makes me so special?" he scolded them. "Because I'm alive?"

Back in court, spectators shifted uneasily in their seats as medical evidence was introduced. A few gasped. Clifford grinded his teeth and bit at his cuticles as he listened. One father in the gallery sat in rapt attention throughout the grisly testimony, holding his three-year-old daughter on his lap.

Reporters watching Geschwendt agreed he looked pale as he listened to the medical testimony, but, talking among themselves later, they said his pallor might not have been due to emotion. It could have been the effect of his limited time in the sun since he was transferred to maximum security.

Jurors' faces twisted when Lieutenant Zajac passed the grotesque color photographs of the bodies to them one at a time, photos so lurid that the judge stipulated no one was allowed to hold one longer than 15 seconds. The 8 × 10s, close-ups of victims shot in the face, were a stark contrast to a color family photo taken a few years earlier with smiling Jack and Peggy Abt standing on either side of their five children, their two clean-cut teenage sons already taller than their father and their older daughter smiling and posing with the self-assurance pretty teenage girls have.

When the judge called a recess, press-shy Clifford exited the courtroom and vanished. Michael hurried into a nearly empty corridor with a bevy of photographers trailing him. A spectator who exited the courtroom immediately behind the brothers turned to her friend and said, "It breaks your heart."

County Detective Dick Batezel was up next. Batezel was such a convincing prosecution witness that new public defenders practiced for trial by pretending they were interrogating a witness like him. Batezel could eat you alive on the stand, one attorney said, because he always answered calmly and competently. Whenever he took the stand, things went the prosecution's way, and the Geschwendt case was no exception.

In his detached monotone, Batezel gave a detailed account of Geschwendt's confession, right down to specific questions Batezel asked and Geschwendt's exact answers, all read directly from the notes Batezel took on the night of the arrest.

The jurors looked visibly shocked when Batezel matter-of-factly mentioned that after Geschwendt confessed to shooting six people, he made an offhand comment that the killings were somewhat of a relief for him because he rarely showed any emotion.

Biehn asked if Geschwendt showed any regrets when he confessed to killing two children and four adults. Batezel, again in his monotone, said, "Yes. He was sorry he couldn't get the other two."

Spectators stiffened in their seats when they heard that, but Biehn knew he didn't have it in the bag yet. To squash an insanity defense, he had to prove Geschwendt knew right from wrong when he committed the murders. "So that's all he said?" Biehn asked.

Suddenly, something felt fishy to Fink. He had scanned the entire confession while he was waiting at the defense table, and it didn't mention Geschwendt saying anything else to Batezel. Fink wasn't sure why, but his instincts kicked in, and he yelled, "Objection."

"A nagging feeling from somewhere rose up in me quite rapidly," Fink recalled. "If George had said nothing more than in the discovery, then why even ask that question?"

The judge called both attorneys to a sidebar. They moved to a spot where jurors couldn't hear them, and the court stenographer lugged his chunky stenograph machine closer to capture their words.

The judge asked Fink what he was objecting to. Fink wanted to know why Biehn asked that question because there was nothing else in the confession he received under court rules. The judge's curiosity was piqued too.

"Did he say anything else?" Judge Beckert asked Biehn.

The answer was a hesitant "yes."

"What?" the judge said.

"Judge, you aren't going to believe this," Biehn said, "but Geschwendt told Batezel that he knew it was wrong when he did it."

Fink said Biehn didn't supply that information to him as required during the discovery phase of the trial, so the jury would never hear it. If they had, it would have sunk his insanity defense.

The DA presented two psychiatrists who said they believed Geschwendt was acutely aware of the difference between right and wrong when he committed the murders, but, on cross-examination, Fink got one of them to say he actually would not disagree that Geschwendt was ill and paranoid.

Biehn needed something to tip the jury. A young man from the neighborhood was a godsend for the prosecutor's case.

Brad Batchelor testified that Geschwendt told him how he faked his way out of the Navy. He said Geschwendt told him he didn't like the Navy at all, but he didn't tell the military psychiatrist that. Instead, Geschwendt just acted quiet whenever the doctor asked him a question, and it worked.

All eyes in the courtroom veered toward Geschwendt, who sat at the defense table just acting quiet. Some spectators' mouths fell open as they made the connection. It seemed the prosecution had clinched it.

Biehn later told reporters that, when his assistant told him Batchelor's story, his first reaction was, "I'm not going to put this guy on the witness stand. Nobody's possibly going to believe that. It was too good to be true." Batchelor tied the case up in a bow for Biehn.

Fink planned to call Geschwendt's mother and siblings to testify about his bullying father and bizarre upbringing, but only one of his five family members was willing, so he had to base his case mainly on psychiatric testimony.

He found two expert witnesses on paranoid schizophrenia, but they both told him they didn't want to testify. He recalled one of them said something like, "Please don't make me do this."

Dr. Ulysses Watson was the director of the Eastern Pennsylvania Psychiatric Institute. Dr. Richard Lonsdorf was a nationally recognized expert on insanity as a legal defense who had developed the law school course on it that was taught to generations of Philadelphia lawyers.

They both told Fink he wasn't going to win the case. Neither of them wanted to testify, but Fink begged them until they relented.

As they were prepping for the trial, Fink asked them if Geschwendt could be cured. They both laughed. "What's funny about that?" he asked. "He would need decades of close, personal, intense psychotherapy, and I wouldn't want to be his therapist," one said. Then they both laughed again. "What's funny about that?" Fink said. One lowered the boom: "He will want to kill whoever gets close to him," he said.

They told Fink that Geschwendt blamed all his problems on the Abts because they were the only people who ever bothered to have a social relationship with him.

In court, Dr. Lonsdorf testified that Geschwendt was paranoid and constantly feared rejection. Jurors looked stunned when he added that the 24-year-old had never touched, kissed or petted any other human being.

Geschwendt was caught up in his insecurities, the doctors said. He thought his nose was too crooked and his voice sounded funny, and he was reluctant to show his hands because he had lost the tips of three fingers in an industrial accident. When his hand was mangled, he blamed the Abts.

He became obsessed with the high-spirited Abts across the street, the doctors testified. Sometimes he dreamed he was friends with them again; other times he dreamed they were in his thrall. It was a true love-hate relationship.

He blamed the Abts when someone started playing practical jokes on him, when the telephone rang and no one was on the other end, when he found trash and rocks on his lawn and when BB pellets peppered his house. He saw Heidi defecate on his lawn, and he thought the Abts were training her to do it.

By Thanksgiving of 1975, Geschwendt believed either the Abts had to go, or he had to go, both doctors said. He believed there was no other way out.

Dr. Watson stunned the courtroom when he said Geschwendt didn't think he'd be sentenced to life imprisonment or the electric chair, even if he were caught, and, if he got 20 years for the six murders, he'd have to consider trying to escape.

The audience was literally taken aback in their chairs when the doctor testified Geschwendt confessed to his mother Josephine Colon on the day after the killings because he felt proud of his accomplishment and wanted to tell someone.

After that stunner, the defense called Mrs. Colon to testify. The instant the pale, gray-haired woman took her seat on the witness stand, she broke into uncontrollable sobs. The judge called a 30-minute recess. When she retook the stand after the recess, she said nothing. She stared absently at the courtroom floor. Her movements exactly mirrored her son's usual posture at the defense table. The judge excused her. As she was escorted from the courtroom, she finally spoke. She loudly announced that she "didn't want any trouble."

The only member of Geschwendt's family willing to testify for him was Betty Kennedy, his 37-year-old sister who had once been an honor student at Bensalem High. The pretty blonde woman came to Doylestown despite the fact that she was in the midst of planning a funeral. She testified her brother George was the shyest and most withdrawn of all four Geschwendt siblings, and she said all four were unusually shy and withdrawn.

Staring at the floor like her mother and brother, she told the jury their childhood home was an unhappy one headed by a dish-throwing, destructive alcoholic father whose four children lived in fear of him. She said he treated all his children the same—"like objects." He chased them with knives. He strung barbed wire around their yard. One of her most vivid childhood memories was the time their father tried to run them all over with his car.

Mrs. Kennedy said she never saw her younger brother show anger or laughter or excitement or any emotion. Fink asked if he ever had any close friends. "Only the Abts," she replied.

Rich Fink closed his case by telling the jurors his client was so mentally ill that he did not know right from wrong. He said nothing proved that more than what his client did minutes after he murdered the only family who had ever befriended him. He went home and made himself a tuna fish sandwich.

Before the jurors left the courtroom, the judge gave them instructions, but he did not fully explain that Geschwendt would be sent to a secure psychiatric facility if they returned a verdict of not guilty by reason of insanity. That one omission sparked 16 years of appeals.

CHAPTER 20

The Verdict

> "George had experienced a real connection with the Abts. When they were gone from his life, his life kept going badly over and over again. And who do you blame when your life goes badly? Well, nobody blames themselves. You blame someone else. The Abts were the only people in his world."
>
> —DEFENSE ATTORNEY RICH FINK

The jurors took only 35 minutes to find Geschwendt guilty of six first-degree murders, less time than they took for their lunch break.

The timing took most people by surprise, including the Abt brothers, who had to be summoned from a local tavern. They were not in the courtroom when Jury Foreman Walter Beretzki read the verdict.

As the jurors took their seats, a young radio reporter sat on the edge of his, bending forward to catch every word as the verdict was announced. A few feet away, Geschwendt sat at the defense table, expressionless. He never looked up. He never locked eyes with his defense attorney. He continued to doodle on a writing pad as the jurors were polled individually:

"Sophie Sams, how you say? Guilty or not guilty as to first-degree murder?"

"Guilty."

Eileen Akers?

"Guilty."

Walter Beretzki?

"Guilty."

David Fell?

"Guilty."

Sandy Harrigan?

"Guilty."

Candace Albert?

"Guilty."

John Rothrock?

"Guilty."

Joan McIlvaine?

"Guilty."

Carol Pollock?

"Guilty."

Bernard Petersen?

"Guilty."

Eleanor Coyne?

"Guilty."

Frederick Smith?

"Guilty."

At the last "guilty," the radio reporter had heard enough. He shot from the courtroom and dashed to a long bank of pay phones to call his station. His loud, clear voice filled the courthouse corridor as he spilled the news into the receiver: "Guilty, guilty, guilty, guilty, guilty, guilty. George Geschwendt was convicted of six counts of first-degree murder …"

It turned out those Bensalem patrolmen assigned to sit in a car in the Abt driveway the week after the murders had been correct. They had half-joked that the killer could be right behind them, watching them as they watched the Abt house. He was. Geschwendt's bedroom with the street-facing window was fewer than 60 feet from the spot where they were parked that night.

The verdict may have reaffirmed Felix Iostracco's faith in his dog's instincts. Early on in the investigation, Iostracco, the Abts' neighbor, told police his dog didn't bark on the night of the murder, and he always barks at strangers.

The jurors had one weighty task to go—deciding whether Geschwendt should be sentenced to life or death. Rich Fink and Ken Biehn each tried their best to sway them. Clifford Abt bit at his stubby fingernails as each attorney had a go at the jurors.

Fink beseeched them to "spare this struggling piece of humanity." He asked the jurors to give Geschwendt the "sympathetic ear" he never had at home. Biehn reminded them how Geschwendt had meticulously planned the slayings. "Somewhere in that sick mind of his, he knew he was wrong," Biehn said.

As the judge gave his final instructions to the jurors before they left to deliberate life or death, Clifford sat in the front row, his fingernails clenched to his lips. When the judge instructed the jurors that they must return a sentence of life imprisonment if they found any mitigating circumstances, Clifford silently but vigorously shook his head "no" several times. He caught the eye of several jurors. I sensed I was watching something extraordinary.

While the jury deliberated, Clifford walked to the opposite end of the courthouse corridor and sat by himself, staring down at the floor. Michael and his friends paced outside the courtroom door like expectant fathers. Reporters stuck around the courtroom too, betting the life-or-death decision would come quickly. They were correct. It took only 95 minutes

As the jurors filed into the courtroom, five deputies straightened themselves to their full height the way cats puff up to appear larger when they sense danger. They lined up between the defense table and the row of seats where the Abts and their friends were sitting.

The gallery fell silent as the clerk asked, "How do you find, death or life in prison?" When the jury foreman said, "Death," spectators gasped aloud. Shoulders stiffened. Mouths actually fell open.

Heads swiveled toward Geschwendt. He kept chewing gum and drawing cars and boxes on a legal pad as if he never heard the foreman speak.

The jury apparently didn't buy the mental illness defense. They went with Ken Biehn's contention that Geschwendt knew he wasn't squashing a beetle when he killed two children and four adults.

Either the jurors thought the crime was just too brutal to be forgiven, or they bought Biehn's characterization of Geschwendt as a cool, calm, collected college graduate who set out to do a job.

While spectators were reeling from the death sentence, Geschwendt kept doodling. He never looked up. He locked eyes with no one. A person's face is not always a good indice of what he is thinking. Maybe he was shocked that his one achievement in life broke badly. Or perhaps he was thinking about what he had told psychiatrist, Dr. Ulysses Watson—that if he got more than 20 years, he might have to think about escaping.

Not one of his family members was there to support him. The only person to cry at the sentence was Rich Fink's young wife, Sandra.

Geschwendt chomped on his gum as the jurors were polled individually. He betrayed no emotion as five men and seven women one by one replied "Death" in uniformly firm voices.

Fink turned to Geschwendt and reassured him they would appeal the verdict. Although to all outward appearances his client looked unruffled, Fink had been around Geschwendt long enough to know that he was scared. "He didn't want to die," Fink said. "The reason I know that is, when they said death penalty, he spoke. He didn't really speak very much, but when I said we're going to appeal, he asked, 'Are they going to kill me in the meantime?'"

Judge Beckert asked Geschwendt if he understood the verdict. He said, "Yes."

The judge ordered Geschwendt to pay $6,755.24 in court costs, but his lawyers would soon file papers showing he would have no prospect of paying at any time in the future.

All of a sudden, as deputies bent to lead the condemned man from his seat, all order in the courtroom evaporated. Glee spread across Edward "Beer Buddy" Myers' face as he hopped up on his one good leg and shouted, "Geschwendt dies!"

A loud cheer rose from the Abts' friends.

Myers and Michael Abt embraced the way Super Bowl fans do when they cheer their team's winning goal.

As their old playmate shuffled out of the courtroom with his hands cuffed, a knot of Abt friends applauded. Two reached over the railing in failed attempts to shake one of Geschwendt's braceleted hands. Some made a "zeep, zeep" noise in unison, mimicking the sound they thought an electric chair would make. One shouted, "Hey, George. You got the hot squat!" Another yelled, "Way to go, George!" Myers chimed in: "Geschwendt will burn in hell."

The five deputies promptly formed a human wall around their prisoner, but a few of his old playmates got so close that Geschwendt instinctively drew his shoulders in as he was whisked from the courtroom.

Even the usually unflappable Judge Beckert seemed to be processing the outlandish scene before him. Young men were making fun of a man who admitted he killed six people because young men had made fun of him.

Reporters rushed up to Clifford, but he declined to comment. Seconds later, flashing a wide smile, he turned to join in the jeering at Geschwendt.

It seemed like a sad final taunt, but, for the first time in the six-day trial, as he passed his old neighbors, Geschwendt smiled ever so slightly.

Flashbulbs popped as he was led into the wide curving corridor towards the main exit. He held his head high, and his face betrayed no emotion as he left the courtroom in the same green shirt and dark pants he had worn to every court appearance.

As he was led outside to a waiting sheriff's car, another set of Abt friends shouted, "George dies!" and "Goodbye, George!" and "How do you like that, baby?" This time, Michael joined in the jeers.

Moments later, the jurors who sentenced Geschwendt to death stopped in their tracks on the sidewalk outside the courthouse. They had been boarding a green sheriff's van to retrieve their things from the Holiday Inn where they had been sequestered. They came to a halt to watch with obvious fascination as the man they had condemned to death was placed in a waiting police car. George Geschwendt was no longer invisible.

The jurors told reporters they made no snap decisions and there were no hysterical speeches in the jury room. They took only two votes on the first-degree murder charge and two on the death penalty.

Rich Fink, who believed Geschwendt desperately needed psychiatric care for paranoid schizophrenia, filed an appeal based on the judge's instructions to the jury regarding an insanity verdict. Appeals lingered in the courts for the next 16 years, but ultimately, they were ill-fated.

The Abt sons said they were satisfied that Geschwendt would die for killing their family, but, as Michael put it, "How can anyone be happy?"

When a Philadelphia reporter asked him if he saw the death sentence as a victory, he said no. He saw it as a debt being paid.

After the trial, Michael's attitude on the death penalty veered. "At that time I was all for it," he said. "Back then, anything went. I was excited. I was happy. I was mad. I was everything. I was angry as shit. As time went by, I felt the longer George lived the more he would suffer. I knew I was in for a lifetime of suffering, so why should he get off easy? Now I think God's the only one who has the right to take a life."

Geschwendt joined four others on Pennsylvania's list of condemned men. Stanton Story killed a policeman. Clifford Futch killed another inmate. Benajmin Davis killed an elderly newsstand operator in the commission of a holdup. Gerald McKenna raped, mutilated and killed a 16-year-old girl.

Bensalem police had a slam-dunk win, but they knew it wouldn't give back any years to 12-year-old Kathy or 13-year-old Johnny. Extracting some measure of justice was the best they could do.

Chief Michaels held a press conference. He gave credit to the detectives. He told reporters there's no feeling of elation or even satisfaction at the end of a case like Geschwendt's, but maybe relief.

Lieutenant Zajac was matter of fact: "We don't come out with the cheerleaders and say we want a guy killed, but this is what you're working for—to have the case cleared."

The police didn't hold a celebration when the case was finally over. Detective Keyser said they were all exhausted.

Inside the courthouse, Ken Biehn attributed the win to "excellent police work," but he admitted the case would have been difficult or even impossible to win if the gun had never turned up or the killer had never confessed.

Both Abt sons congratulated Biehn and thanked him. The DA had two reasons to celebrate that week. He won the trial, and the county commissioners voted him a $26,000 raise.

As the detectives' job was winding up, work was just beginning at area newspapers. I typed my story on CompuScan paper, heavyweight white typing paper with bright-red margins. Women in the newspaper's back shop fed the thick pages through an electronic scanner that replaced the silver-colored, hot metal type seen in old newspaper movies.

Our front-page hed was "Geschwendt is Given Death Penalty." The lead on the story was "George Geschwendt got a round of applause last night as he left the courtroom after being sentenced to death for the March 12 murder of five members of the John Abt family and a family friend."

Headline writers across the country summed up the unprecedented day in court with "Crowd Taunts Doomed Man" and "Death Times Six for Abt Murderer" and "Sadist Butcher Gets Hot Seat." The last one was plastered across the front page of the *Yardley News*, a small weekly paper from the opposite end of Bucks County.

A tabloid writer from Philadelphia noted that Geschwendt finally achieved the one thing he wanted all his life—to be somebody—but he did so over the bodies of six people.

Meanwhile, in Trevose, where they referred to the mass murder as "what happened" or "it," the question on every neighbor's lips that day was, "What did he get for it?" Most seemed relieved by the answer.

When one woman heard the jurors dealt six death sentences to Geschwendt, she said Geschwendt dealt six life sentences to Clifford and Michael. They would spend the rest of their lives without their parents, their sisters, their younger brother or their friend, she said.

Ed Simpson, a friend of Geschwendt and the Abts, said Geschwendt's arrest had come as a complete surprise to him, but he thought the death penalty was fair. "He deserves it," Simpson said. "You can't run around doing that and get away with it."

"Whatever they do to him, it's too good," said a neighbor who remembered holding Kathy and Johnny in her arms when they were babies.

Geschwendt's singular act had an extraordinary negative reach beyond Michael and Clifford. He had left his six victims' best friends and godchildren and work friends adrift—from the 14-year-old cousin who repeatedly phoned Kathy Abt on her last night, to the Boy Scouts who depended on Jack Abt to lead the local troop.

Michael slept a solid 12 hours on the evening of July 19, his first good night's sleep since March 11. He said the last thing he thought about when he went to bed at night was what the killer told the police—that he was the one Geschwendt disliked most. That was also the first thing he thought about when he woke the next morning. "Sometimes I feel if he had gotten me, maybe the rest of my family might still be around," he said.

Michael told reporters he understood that Rich Fink believed that he was correct when he told the jurors Geschwendt wasn't legally responsible for the killings because of his paranoid schizophrenia. It still irked him, though. "I'm just curious as to what Mr. Fink would do with me and my brother if we were to find we couldn't fit into a normal life. He's so concerned about Geschwendt. I don't see any concern coming our way about how we're adjusting," he said. "Who's the victim and who's the criminal here?"

The *Courier Times* ran an editorial: "What went wrong in Geschwendt's mind? How can it be averted in the future?"

"Some people are too flawed to handle life," Rich Fink said decades later. "That's what my closing to the jury should have been. What do we do with those people who are too fragile? We should show them the compassion that Jesus taught us. Or something."

"George had experienced a real connection with the Abts. When they were gone from his life, his life kept going badly over and over again," Fink said. "And who do you blame when your life goes badly? Well, nobody blames themselves. You blame someone else. The Abts were the only people in his world."

CHAPTER 21

The Afterparty

> Picnic tables and a barbecue grill were set up near the door where Geschwendt had broken in.

The Abt brothers hosted a party at their home to celebrate the trial's end. After five torturous months of police probes and court dates, the mood that night was buoyant.

Clifford and Michael both brought their fiancées. It was 80 degrees and humid, but there were smiles all around. If their summer could have been captured in a single freezeframe, this would be as good as it got.

The party at the murder scene wrapped a heartbreaking trial with crime scene photos so lurid no juror was allowed to view them for more than 15 seconds. Everyone there knew the verdict would not turn things right side up again. Michael's and Clifford's futures would still be skewed by the killings. Geschwendt's house, visible from the picnic tables, was a permanent bleak reminder of what had happened, but that night was a forward-looking celebration.

George Geschwendt was a shadow over their lives that could never fade. But, that night, they were laughing and smiling and surrounded by friends in their family home. Picnic tables and a barbecue grill were set up near the door where Geschwendt had broken in. Young men with nicknames like Beer Buddy surrounded Clifford and Michael. Many of them had been friends since the Abts moved to Trevose when Michael was 10 and Clifford was 12.

I was seated at a picnic table talking to a soft-spoken, long-haired man who was about my age when Clifford approached and asked me to help him with something. He led me a distance from the picnic table, bent his lanky body to get closer to my ear, and quietly advised me to change seats because the man I was sitting next to was crazy. I told him we were just talking, and the guy seemed nice. Positioning his shoulder to block anyone from overhearing, he leaned in again and brought his voice down another notch. In a tone that veered toward urgency, he said the man had recently tried to kill himself. When I said sometimes people get depressed and even attempt suicide, he leaned in further and said, "With a machete?" I found another seat.

★★★

Geschwendt, who called his childhood home his concentration camp, was off to a real prison. Graterford, the state's largest maximum-security prison, housed 1,698 men in 1976. It was surrounded by a three-story stone wall topped with nine guard towers.

★★★

The Abt house looks much different than it did in 1976. The two-story traditional home has changed hands several times since the murders. It last sold for $415,000 in 2021, before the housing prices shot up.

Whenever a home sale included an open house, some neighbors would attend to see what the sellers did with the basement.

One owner remodeled it as a family room with a full bathroom and a laundry area. The real estate brochure boasted that it would make a perfect in-law suite. "They didn't say anything about anybody dying in there," one neighbor noted.

Under Pennsylvania law, home sellers must reveal a leaky water heater or a problem with the downspouts, but there is no legal requirement to offer information about a house's lethal history.

Certainly, there was no heads-up for the couple who unwittingly bought the site of the 1967 Mary Mamon murder in nearby Levittown.

The unsuspecting buyer said his house was priced slightly lower than other homes on his gently winding street, but that didn't raise a red flag for him. "We just thought it was a fixer-upper type of house. It was all dark. The paneling was from the '70s. It had the original '50s cabinets. It needed an upgrade," he said.

His first inkling that something was amiss came during the couple's first Easter season there. Someone left a flower arrangement on their front walk on Holy Thursday 2002, exactly 35 years after Mrs. Mamon beat Lorraine Mullery to death and bludgeoned two children there.

"We thought they were Easter flowers," the homeowner said. "There was no card or anything. We didn't think much of it." The couple didn't put all the clues together until their seven-year-old grandson came to visit two years later. "He went up the street to play, and a neighbor kid said, 'You live in the murder house.' That's how we came to find out," the homeowner said. His wife hastily checked the internet. The playmate was correct. They had purchased a house that neighborhood children once crossed the street to avoid.

"We couldn't move, financially, because, by the time we found out, the houses here had almost doubled in price," he said. "I'm a practical person. My wife's practical too. It is what it is."

He said they explored a lawsuit, but it didn't pan out: "I'm somewhat of an opportunist," he said. "I thought, 'They didn't tell me. Maybe I can make some money off it.' But I called a lawyer, and he said it's the law."

The producers of a national television show about haunted houses came knocking at their door and were turned away.

Some houses where adverse events happen actually sell for over asking price. Real estate agents say memories fade and a good house in a good neighborhood with good schools always sells.

CHAPTER 22

Spree Shooter Kills Six

New York City's notorious spree killer the Son of Sam killed six victims, the same number as Geschwendt.

After the trial, things slowly began to go back to normal for everyone in Trevose except George Geschwendt's family and Michael and Clifford Abt, who were gravely shortchanged.

Within 10 days after the Abt trial, national attention turned toward another spree killer. On July 29, two women were sitting in a double-parked Oldsmobile in the Pelham Bay section of the Bronx when a man approached their car and fired three bullets. One woman was injured; the other was killed instantly. It was the first of the murders attributed to David Berkowitz, who would become known as the Son of Sam, a New York City legend in the '70s.

Headline writers first called the shooter "the .44-Caliber Killer," but, eventually, over his 13-month killing spree, he named himself Son of Sam. He wrote letters claiming a black Labrador Retriever belonging to his neighbor, Sam Carr, ordered him to spill the blood of attractive young women. Years later, he admitted he had made the whole thing up.

Everybody everywhere was talking about Son of Sam, including two of his victims. Judy Placido, 17, and her 20-year-old boyfriend, Salvatore Lupo, were actually discussing the shootings in a parked car outside a Queens discotheque when a stocky White man appeared at their driver's side window and fired four shots at them. The wounded couple leapt out of the car and headed for the safety of the discotheque. They both survived.

Females with long, dark hair were Son of Sam's most frequent targets. The killings went on long enough that women began cutting their hair short and dyeing it blond.

I unexpectedly wound up in New York City on July 14, 1977, while Son of Sam was still on the loose, but that never occurred to me or my colleague. We were following another story almost as big. A blackout had hit New York City the previous night. Looters broke windows and set stores on fire. It was the first blackout since the original Great Northeast Blackout hit 10 states and parts of Canada in 1965.

A photographer I worked with was looking for someone accustomed to driving in New York City so he could get some historic shots. Manhattan was fewer than two hours away from our newsroom. I was game.

I experienced the first blackout from afar when I was a teenager in rural New Jersey. My borough of 501 residents didn't change much when the lights went out. Twelve years later, I thought it would be fun to see how Times Square looked once the ribbon of news headlines stopped circling the Allied Chemical Tower.

Without electricity, the five-foot-high ribbon was a plain black strip. The three-story-high head of a Winston cigarette smoker that loomed over Times Square for decades wasn't blowing his usual 1,000 huge smoke rings a day because the steam-producing box behind it had no juice.

On Madison Avenue, more people were carrying flashlights than briefcases. New Yorkers were strolling across Broadway like it was a country road. Cars were stuck in the underbellies of parking garages whose elevators had stalled.

We saw some smashed windows, but the most severe thefts were in other parts of the city.

Before we left, I wondered what subways would be like in the pitch dark. I descended the gritty steps to the 42nd Street subway station at Times Square. It got darker with every step. I forced myself to keep walking because I wanted to see what total darkness would look like on a subway platform. When I reached the bottom, I couldn't see even an inch in front of me. It was pitch black. I couldn't tell if anyone was next to me. If I remembered the platform configuration correctly, the tracks would have to be a couple yards away, but I wasn't certain. I turned around and raced up to the street level as fast as I could. When I told the photographer, he laughed. He told me he had tried the same thing earlier, and he lasted about the same amount of time.

Neither of us thought of Son of Sam, even on the long ride back to Bucks County. He was back in the papers the next day, though, because the anniversary of the first shooting was coming up on July 29.

On the last day of July, Berkowitz shot a couple kissing in a parked car. He killed the woman, blinded her date, and extended his terrifying grip on a city of eight million.

He was still on the loose in the city when I was doing a routine feature story about a retired NYPD officer who had just been hired as police chief of Morrisville, Pennsylvania, a small Bucks County town. I needed a good lead for my feature story on him, so I asked if he knew anything about the Son of Sam case. It turned out he was friends with Inspector Timothy Dowd, who was heading up the search. He said they were closer to an arrest than it appeared.

He predicted Son of Sam would be behind bars before summer was out. He told me the gunman probably was Jewish or Italian because all his shootings were in ethnic neighborhoods, and anyone who looked too different would stick out like a sore thumb. He said any killer who could evade capture for nearly a year probably could fade in with the crowd.

He was correct. Berkowitz was nabbed six days later. By the time he was apprehended, he had killed six victims, the same number as Geschwendt.

CHAPTER 23

The Aftermath

The Vogenberger murders remain a double mystery, but police did find some of the cash the killers were after. To do it, they enlisted a Delaware psychic.

When the Historic Langhorne Association presented a taped travelogue narrated by the late Ed Vogenberger in the fourth week of 1977, the Vogenberger murder case had already gone cold. It was included in a newspaper series on unsolved murders.

★★★

By the time George Geschwendt was sentenced for the Abt murders in the summer of 1976, Pennsylvania's oak-stained electric chair sat in pieces in an unoccupied cell in the basement of the State Correctional Institution at Rockview, alongside broken beds and spare machinery. The death chamber had been converted to office space. The wires that supplied 2,000 volts of electricity and the large canopy used to vent fumes during electrocutions were still in place, though.

When a tabloid reporter told Michael Abt the chair was sitting in pieces in storage, Michael offered to put it together himself, and he added that he would be willing to pull the switch, too. "In fact, I would be disappointed if they didn't ask me to do it," he said.

The chair, nicknamed Old Smokey, had been used 350 times between 1915 and 1962. The first person to sit in it was John Talap in 1915, who killed his wife. One of the 12 witnesses was his father-in-law. The last person to die in the chair was Elmo Smith, who raped and murdered a 16-year-old Manayunk girl he abducted as she was on her way home from the movies at Christmastime 1959. After 1976, there were just three executions in the state, all by lethal injection.

In the two years after the jury sentenced Geschwendt to death, public sentiment began to swing against the death penalty. Prosecutors in Bucks County moved swiftly to assure Geschwendt stayed put amid a swirl of court rulings on the constitutionality of the death sentences. To hedge their bets, they brought Geschwendt back to the Bucks County Courthouse for another layer of sentencing in the summer of 1978. Six consecutive life sentences were added on top of his half-dozen death sentences.

The Abt brothers were not in attendance, but about 50 people turned out to watch the proceedings. Several noted that Geschwendt had traded his green shirt for a brown prison-issue one worn with brown slacks.

When Judge Beckert asked if Geschwendt had anything to say before sentencing, the killer made his first lengthy public pronouncement. He announced that he had found Jesus.

"I'd like to say that, since I have been in prison, I accepted Jesus Christ as my personal Lord and Savior," he said excitedly. "I have become a Christian now and a believer. I am sure that the Lord God, through penance, has accepted me as a child of God. He loves us all the same. I know that man may not forgive me, but I know that God has. We have all sinned ..."

He stopped abruptly.

Judge Beckert asked if he was finished. "I did not mean to interrupt you," he said.

"I thought you said to stop," Geschwendt answered.

"No, you may continue," the judge said.

"I was saying that we have all sinned, and we must come before the glory of God through repentance. He's accepted me as a child of God, and he loves us all the same."

Geschwendt said he was praying for the Abts.

Judge Becker let him finish. As soon as he did, the judge imposed six death sentences and six life sentences. He told Geschwendt he had a right to appeal.

Rich Fink told reporters Geschwendt was passing his time in prison reading the Bible. "Religious life is the most important thing to him now," Fink said. "He's searching for salvation for what he's done."

The headline writer at *The Morning Call* in Allentown, Pennsylvania, summed it up, "Bucks Murderer Finds God—Also Draws Six Life Terms."

Geschwendt's attorneys announced he no longer had any animosity toward the Abts. The reverse was not true.

When Clifford Abt heard Geschwendt had found religion, he said, "His heart might belong to Jesus, but his ass still belongs to me and Michael."

When Michael heard, he said, "If he wants to talk to God, let me send him on his way."

While Michael and Clifford were adjusting to life on their own, Geschwendt was having his own problems adjusting to life in prison. He got into a fight with prison guards at Graterford and suffered a head wound severe enough to require stitches. The guards said the 150-pound prisoner attacked them. He spent eight months in solitary confinement. While he was in solitary, Geschwendt missed a chance to see a classmate from the Bensalem High Class of 1970. When Patrolman Bill Fox visited Graterford on a police tour, he looked around for Geschwendt. He wondered whether he'd remember him from math class.

Geschwendt's visitor card had no names on it when his new public defender, Seth Weber, visited him in 1979. He did not have a single visitor in three years, although he was from a family of six and the prison was less than an hour's drive from Trevose.

Seth Weber and Stuart Wilder, his attorneys, said Geschwendt's mental illness was more apparent in 1979 than it had been at his trial three years earlier. He looked like he was on tranquilizers, but he wasn't. He complained that he could hear the other prisoners reading his mind. Whenever he talked about it, his deep voice would suddenly become squeaky and high-pitched.

When the lawyers visited Geschwendt with the good news that they could get his death penalties vacated so he would not be put to death, he displayed no emotion. "We're talking to him, and he keeps looking off to the side at the clock in the room," Weber said. "After about 15 minutes, Stu says, 'I'm sorry, George. Are we keeping you from something? You keep looking at the clock. Do you have somewhere else to be?' This was George's reason: 'I go to some classes here, and there is a class on the weather. I've been to a couple and I really enjoyed them and I don't want to miss it. It starts at 11.'" "We're trying to tell him we think we can get his death penalty vacated and he's not going to die. But he has a class on the weather that he doesn't want to miss," Weber said. "This was a guy who was not in his right mind, no question."

★★★

Years later, Fink said, Geschwendt wrote to District Attorney Ken Biehn asking him to put him to death. He was 41 and he was serving six life sentences with no possibility of parole.

By the time Geschwendt mailed his letter, the prosecutor had long since moved on. Just before Christmas in 1979, newspapers ran a photo of him being sworn in as a judge on the Court of Common Pleas. The other man in the photo was a smiling Judge Paul Beckert, the judge who presided over Geschwendt's trial.

The arc of Geschwendt's life was unchanged.

The *Weekly World News*, the supermarket tabloid that ran headlines like "Gluten Killed the Dinosaurs," featured Geschwendt's case in an April 1991 issue. The story dubbed Michael Abt a "beer-drinking bruiser" and called Geschwendt a "skinny weirdo serving six life terms." The story ran next to a quiz headlined, "Are You an Emotional Eater? Answer These Questions and Find Out."

Three decades after he broke into the Abt home, Geschwendt was mentioned on two episodes of TV's fictional *Criminal Minds* series—one in 2011 and one in 2015.

In "The Bittersweet Science," a 2011 episode, the FBI's behavioral analysis unit investigates a tidy spree killer in Philadelphia. Dr. Spencer Reid, a character with eidetic memory, rattles off information about Geschwendt cleaning up his crime scenes to avoid detection.

Geschwendt isn't mentioned by name in 2015's "A Place at the Table," but the online entertainment platform Fandom lists him as the inspiration for the episode's central character, a spree killer who targets families out of revenge.

★★★

Police officers who worked the Abt and Vogenberger murders were familiar with every street on their beat, but the landmarks in the back of their minds are more complicated than most passersby's. While another driver might see a photo studio, a patrol officer might recall it as the scene of a bludgeoning. A local bank to some might be an armed robbery site to them. A model home might be a murder scene. The Abt and Geschwendt houses will always be memorable to the band of police officers who solved a baffling mass murder in 10 days.

Recollections about the case sometimes become fuzzy when retired officers meet for lunch or golf or reconnect for special occasions. Detectives and uniformed officers say their mouths sometimes drop when they hear another member of the force recalling how he played a role in the case that they actually played. One said he thinks to himself, "Wait. Were you even in the room?"

★★★

The Vogenberger murders remain a double mystery, but police did find some of the cash the killers were after.

To do it, they enlisted a Delaware psychic. Her standard fee was two steak dinners—one for herself and one for her spouse.

The woman, who had consulted with several police departments, told the detectives she bases her revelations on people's auras. "Every once in a while there is a freak of nature born who has the ability to see this color or aura that surrounds every animate and inanimate object. In 1944, I was lucky enough to be one of those people who were born with it," she said. "I can only be used as an investigative aid. A female Dick Tracy I ain't. I don't try and play police."

She laid down three ground rules: First, if she gave them useful information, they would all go out for a steak dinner, and she could take her husband along. Second, they should select the detective who knew the most about the case to hand her photos of the victims. She would talk directly to him. And she told them, "If I catch you pacifying me or patronizing me, I will become terribly temperamental, as that would be an insult to my intelligence."

Holding a photo of Ed Vogenberger, she said the balding, ruddy-faced farmer was independent, stubborn, strong-willed, highly opinionated and a loner who was not overly communicative. He was somewhat frugal and had a little store of money that no one was aware of, she said.

Holding a photo of Marguerite, a plump, gray-haired retired bank clerk primly dressed and wearing sensible shoes, she pegged her as a loner who was "strong with her mouth." She said she had hidden some money.

The couple was wealthy, but frugal, the psychic said. They invested in stocks and kept very careful records of their investments. If police could take the farmhouse apart piece by piece, they would find thousands of dollars, she said.

She said all the Vogenbergers' outbuildings had things hidden in them. She told them to look behind an electric outlet.

Acting on her advice, police searched a barn where a Vogenberger relative had told them the couple sometimes hid cash. They had searched there before, but turned up nothing. This time, a detective felt around behind an electrical outlet box as the psychic had suggested. His fingers hit two small tin boxes. He found a stack of $20 bills in one and a stack of tens in another for a total haul of $3,810. It appeared the Vogenbergers never gave up at least one of their hiding places.

The Vogenberger case took detectives to Texas, California and North Carolina interviewing anyone who might shed light on the killings, including a person connected to a gun used in the murders.

Mather, the lead detective, had two favorite suspects. The police chief had two favorites of his own. Neither had enough evidence for an arrest. It remains a baffling puzzle 50 years later, but the case has not been forgotten. Anyone with information can call Bucks County Detectives at 215 348 6354.

David Hanks, a cold case detective who retired in 2024, said time sometimes helps solve cases. As relationships change and dangerous criminals die, people who have information are more likely to come forward.

Hanks' favorite suspects were Frank Tomlinson and John Dickel, the same men Detective Mather liked for it in 1976. Both are deceased. He said Tomlinson made more sense than anyone else because he was a relative with a violent past. He knew where the farmhouse was. He knew the victims. He knew the area. And he would bring the Tasers because he'd likely know he'd have to torture the thrifty couple to get their money.

Hanks said the just-the-facts nature of police reports works against a cold case detective reading reports decades later. Each detective through the years carries his own theory of the crime in the back of his mind, but rule number one of police reports is it is a report, just the facts, not a narrative. Since suspicions are not facts, a detective who comes along a half century later has no idea why the original detective favored one suspect over another.

CHAPTER 24

Sad Shared Memories

> One woman who was haunted by the Abt murders throughout her childhood is approaching 65 now, but she said still flinches whenever her family is away and she has to enter her home alone.

Like the façade of the Abt home, much has changed in Bucks County since 1976, but the people who lived through the Abt murders still remember it as a milestone as etched in their memories as any national historic event.

Gary Mitchell was sitting in a bar one day when a man asked when the Abts were killed. In a split second, Mitchell answered, "March 12, 1976." The other guy was incredulous. Mitchell, who was 12 when the murders happened, told the guy to look it up on his phone. Mitchell was on the nose. "It's instilled in my mind. I remember it like it was yesterday," he said. "I lost two good friends that day."

"It's like when we landed on the moon," said Marianne Seborowski McGinnis, who grew up in Trevose. "Anybody you talk to who has been here forever always remembers the Abt murders. You remember because nothing like that ever happened here."

One woman who was haunted by the case throughout her childhood is approaching 65 now, but she said still flinches whenever her family is away and she has to enter her home alone.

Memories of the 10-day search for the killer are fading five decades later, but people still talk about the what-ifs on a night when every minute mattered.

What if Michael had arrived home on time and had become the seventh victim? Dave Clee probably would have driven his patrol car past the Abt house uninterrupted and unaware, like Ted Baker and Dot Lombardo and Carole Ebersole and the Sears deliveryman.

Or what would have happened if the killer were still in place behind the living room wall when Officer Clee walked into the kitchen sometime after 8 p.m.? Geschwendt told the detectives he wouldn't have hesitated to kill a police officer.

What if Margie Abt had kept walking with the telephone in her hand?

Maria D'Ambrosio, the papergirl, came within 20 feet of the killer. What if John Abt had paid her for his newspaper inside, as he had every other week?

What if the vile atmosphere in the Geschwendt home never caused ripples of misery beyond its walls?

What if Fred Geschwendt Sr. had not bullied and starved and terrorized his wife and four children? What if he gave up drinking and spent his paycheck on food to feed his family?

What if George Geschwendt had the social skills to thwart the young bullies who picked on him?

What if he had been treated with kindness and understanding from his birth until the day in November 1975 when he decided to kill the Abt family?

What if he had a job to occupy his thoughts and lift his spirits? Forty-five percent of mass shooters are unemployed.

What if Judy King had quit phoning Kathy Abt? It was the constantly ringing phone that put Geschwendt on edge and prompted him to leave the house less than 15 minutes before Michael Abt arrived.

What if Jack and Peggy Abt had lived to enjoy their family?

What if Michael and Clifford Abt had not had their family's love stolen from them?

When the adults who lived through those harrowing days in Trevose talk about what Clifford Abt called "this thing that happened," several of them volunteer one lesson from the murders that stuck in their minds through the decades. One after another after another, they mention that they reared their children to always treat others kindly. As one woman put it, "After that, I always said to my kids always be nice to everyone. You never know."

As defense attorney Rich Fink said, time bombs surround us and we hope parents, teachers, friends and neighbors spot them so they can be helped and defused.

Split-level homes have grown up in the farm fields that once lined both sides of hilly Dara Faith Drive. Bensalem, the township that surrounds it all, is now the ninth most populous locale in Pennsylvania.

The thing that happened almost 50 years ago is mostly forgotten by the general public, but the slip of a name or a chance glimpse of a house pulls people right back to it.

For a man who rides with his wife as she delivers food for DoorDash, that happens every time they turn onto Fleetwood Avenue: "Even to this day, when we drive by the house, we'll say, "That's where the Abts lived," he said. "And then we'll point to the other side and say, "That's where Geschwendt lived."

Epilogue

Michael Abt lives in Bucks County.

***

Clifford Abt died on August 30, 1989. He was 37. He was married and had one stepdaughter. He worked as a machine operator in Levittown. One line in his obituary said, "Mr. Abt's parents, sisters and brother were victims of a mass murder in 1976."

***

George Geschwendt died of natural causes on May 22, 2020, long after his massacre had faded from the headlines. His death was not reported in the newspapers. Neither Michael Abt nor the police officers who worked the case were notified of his death.

In his last prison mug shot, Geschwendt looked much different than the scrawny 24-year-old who broke into the Abt house. His head was shaved. His thin brush moustache was gone. His signature wire-rimmed glasses were missing. His most noticeable facial features were two thick, dark eyebrows, so arched that they looked like black half-moons.

He put on 20 pounds in prison, placing him at the top of the healthy weight range for his five-foot-eight-inch frame. He would likely no longer fit in the hiding place he used 44 years earlier.

At the time of his death from sepsis, he was Inmate AM1851 at the State Correctional Institution at Waymart in the northeastern corner of Pennsylvania, about 150 miles from Trevose. He was 68.

***

Chief Larry Michaels left the police department after a successful run for county sheriff on the Republican ticket in 1981. He was reelected five times. He served until 2002 when he retired due to his health. He died in 2005.

***

Lieutenant Ted Zajac, who ran the Abt murders investigation, became chief of police in Bensalem in 1985. He retired in 1988. He died in 2024.

***

Detective Bob Eckert left the Bensalem Police Department in 1986. He worked as a supervisory special agent for the U.S. Department of State. He retired as assistant director of its Bureau of Diplomatic Security in 2010. He lives in Florida.

***

Detective Ed Keyser retired in 1994 as a detective sergeant. He lives in Los Angeles.

***

Bill Fox, who worked as a police dispatcher during the Abt investigation, became a Bensalem patrolman in 1979. In 1990, the Jaycees chose him as the outstanding law enforcement officer in Pennsylvania for his service record and his fundraising work for children's charities. He retired in 2005. Fox sat between Clifford Abt and George Geschwendt in math class at Bensalem High. Six years later, they would all become involved in the murder case—Clifford as a survivor, Bill as a police dispatcher and George as the doer.

***

Patrolman Dave Clee, who found the bodies on his dinner break, served 29 years on the Bensalem police force, working on the department's plainclothes tactical squad, and joining a drug task force as a special Bucks County detective.

He made what may be the country's first arrest of a Catholic priest in an indecent assault on a child case. Clee was on routine patrol in Trevose on a pleasant summer night in 1982 when he noticed an oddly positioned car in the parking lot of the Northeast Hilton. It seemed angled to afford an unobstructed view of the X-rated movies showing in the neighboring Lincoln Drive-In Theater. When he approached the car, Clee saw Reverend Robert Hermley with two boys aged 13 and 14. There were 14 pornographic magazines in his car. Hermley, a guidance counselor at a Catholic high school in Delaware, pleaded guilty to indecent assault, indecent exposure, open lewdness and corrupting the morals of minors. He was sentenced to three years' probation.

Although the widely publicized case of Reverend Gilbert Gauthe, a Louisiana priest who admitted to abusing more than three dozen children, brought the issue of abuse by priests to the headlines, the Hermley prosecution occurred three years earlier.

Clee retired from the Bensalem Township Police Department in 2002. Before he did, the township honored its police officers with bubblegum-style baseball cards. Clee's card included his favorite quote from Davy Crockett: "Be sure you're right. Then go ahead."

Clee and his wife, Donna, the nurse who cared for Michael Abt in the immediate aftermath of the slayings, still live on Fleetwood Avenue.

***

Bob Hickey, who helped drain the Abts' pool and carry the body of their dog, Heidi, on that March 12 weekend, was a long-time volunteer in Trevose with the fire company and the rescue squad. He died in 2023.

***

Decades after the murders, Maria D'Ambrosio Bryant, the Abts' one-time newspaper carrier, said she didn't realize in 1976 how lucky she was that day. "Thank God Mr. Abt paid me out there, that he had the money on him," she said.

Bryant married and raised her family in the Trevose area. After retirement, the Bryants moved to the New Jersey shore.

★★★

County Detective Dick Batezel, who structured the peak-tension test that led to Geschwendt's confession, died in 2000. When he died, Rich Fink wrote a letter to the editor lauding him, even though the confession Batezel coaxed nixed Fink's chances of winning his first murder case.

Fink's gracious letter said that he was grateful for men like Batezel and "the army of anonymous men like him who protect people like us while we sleep."

★★★

Ken Biehn, the district attorney appointed to the county bench, became president judge of the Bucks County Court of Common Pleas. He retired in 2007. Before he did, he wrote a manual for future prosecutors on how to approach a murder case when an insanity defense is expected.

★★★

Rich Fink, Geschwendt's public defender, became the county's chief public defender a year after the Abt trial. In 1980, he went on to a successful private law practice. Although he was no longer their supervisor, public defenders still sought his advice. "Even after he left the office, we all used to go to him for advice and talk with him. He was such a tactician, and he always had time for us," Stuart Wilder said. "I looked up to him, and I always wanted to impress him, because he was such a leader in the criminal bar here."

Fink, who worked indefatigably on behalf of his client in 1976, continued to work on behalf of mentally ill defendants in Pennsylvania as a volunteer with the Pennsylvania Association of Criminal Defense Lawyers.

★★★

Judge Paul Beckert, who presided over the Mary Mamon trial and the Geschwendt case, went on to helm another sensational case before his retirement in 1989.

In 1977, he presided over the Connie Harman murder case. Harman, a prominent civic leader and a suburban mother of four, shot her lover at the Mall Motel in Bensalem, the same motel where George Geschwendt's mother worked as a cleaner. Harman wrapped the body in the motel's purple shower curtain and phoned her 19-year-old daughter to help her dispose of it. Harman's attorney presented an early battered-woman defense. She was acquitted.

Judge Beckert died in 2011.

★★★

Joseph Hennessey, who murdered Officer Jimmy Armstrong in 1975, spent the next 47 years in the Pennsylvania prison system. He died there in 2022.

★★★

Mike Renshaw, the *Courier Times* reporter who wrote the Hennessey script idea for the *Rosetti and Ryan* television show, became editor-in-chief of the *Courier Times* in the 1980s. Later, he worked at KYW-TV in Philadelphia and launched The Newschannel, a pioneering cable network.

He wrote a song about the Troubles in Northern Ireland with Peter Yarrow of Peter, Paul and Mary. In 2013, he wrote *Mary Travers: A Woman's Words*, a biography of singer Mary Travers. He died in 2019.

★★★

Middletown Detective Donald Mather, lead on the Vogenberger murders, became a Bucks County detective and then deputy chief detective for Bucks County. He died in 2018 aged 77.

★★★

Ten years after the Vogenbergers' farmhouse and acreage were sold, a group of residents raised enough money to buy the farm and preserve it as open space. It remains a treasure within the borough limits. Concerts are staged outdoors there. Each summer about 100 people tend community garden plots. Ten artist studios occupy the outbuildings. One artist reportedly paints Marguerite Vogenberger into her paintings.

Acknowledgements

I hope this book captures the everyday heroes and the real villains of Fleetwood Avenue.

I hope, too, that a reader might have information that would be helpful in solving the 50-year-old cold case of Edward and Marguerite Vogenberger, who were shot to death during the same hours the Abts were killed.

Many of the people I thank here have one thing in common—a connection with six horrific slayings that shook us all in the mid-1970s, when multiple murders still jolted Americans.

I never would have thought of writing about the Abt family murders if three friends from the *Bucks County Courier Times*, my first newspaper, hadn't suggested it. Retired reporters Mary Ellen Bornak, Carl La Vo and Pat Wandling were kind enough to show up at a book signing for my second book at a Barnes & Noble store in Bucks County. We began reminiscing, and they suggested I should tell the story of the Abt murders that I covered in 1976. After a trip back to the street where it happened, I realized they were right.

Writing this book has been like riding a time machine to the '70s and visiting with people I liked then. It was unbelievably enjoyable to reconnect with Michael Abt, Ed Allahand and Dave and Donna Clee on the same day in 2022 after 46 years. I could not have written the same book without Ed's and Dave's help.

Ed's knowledge of Trevose in the 1970s is comprehensive—from kids' games to the types of trees that grew there.

Dave, with his deep knowledge of Trevose and his 29 years on the police force, helped in countless ways. I'm grateful to him and Donna

Clee for their time and their many kindnesses. They both added immensely to the story.

I am grateful to Michael Abt, who was robbed of so much in 11 hours, for taking the time to confirm my memories of events that happened in March and August of 1976.

Defense Attorney Rich Fink's vivid recollections and his frank reflections on the Geschwendt case were invaluable to me in putting together a picture of what happened in Doylestown in the summer of 1976. I can't thank him enough. I'm also grateful to attorneys Seth Weber and Stuart Wilder.

I am grateful to Judge Matthew D. Weintraub and Assistant District Attorney Edward Louka for their help. Without their kindness, there might not have been a book about this case.

Bob Eckert, a Bensalem detective who became assistant director at the U.S. Department of State's Bureau of Diplomatic Security, told me that, when he was first deciding on a career path, someone told him that, if he became a police officer, he'd always have great stories to tell when he retired. He certainly does.

So do the other Bensalem officers and their wives. I am grateful to all of them for filling in the blanks in the story with first-hand accounts—Paige Berry, Dave Clee, Donna Clee, Lenora Dechant, Bob Eckert, Lucy Edwards, Bill Fox, Nancy Fox, Ed Keyser, Pat Zajac and the late Ted Zajac. The police officers had exciting jobs that they loved, and their lively memories add immeasurably to the book.

As I was researching, it dawned on me that a band of fewer than 10 detectives and the patrolmen who worked with them solved a sextuple murder in 10 days with no fingerprints, no witnesses, no cameras, no DNA, no street cameras or doorbell cameras or national computer databases. Although the book is based on records, the best parts came directly from the people who were on Fleetwood Avenue during those 10 days in March 1976. I'm thankful so many were so generous with their time and so willing to help.

In addition to the police officers, the members of the Trevose Fire Company added much to this story, especially Marianne Seborowski McGinnis and the late Bob Hickey.

In Trevose, I was fortunate to meet Ted Baker, Kristie Biedrzycki, Maria D'Ambrosio Bryant, John Gottschalk, Karen Hickey, Reverend Don Keller, Gary Mitchell, Martin Surgoft and the patrons of Carmen's Place. I'm grateful for the memories they shared and their generous introductions to others. I'm especially thankful to Cathy Urban Demi, Margie Abt's best friend, for taking so much time to share her contacts and her photos of Margie.

I also thank Dr. Bill Haney, Peggy Abt's nephew, for sharing his family photos of happier times.

I am grateful to Katherine Nobles at Archbishop Wood High School and Ray Guim of the Bensalem High School Alumni Association. I was fortunate to meet them, albeit only by email. They went out of their way to help a writer they didn't know.

It was a pleasure to meet James Bogan at Bensalem Country Club; Mike Brill, the township treasurer, and Dawn Davis and Mayor Joseph DiGirolamo in the mayor's office. Thanks, too, to Kathleen Leighton, Carolyn Per and Sally Sondesky at the Historical Society of Bensalem Township.

I thank Tony Maniscola, retired special agent at the Pennsylvania Attorney General's Office for his help.

At the Bucks County Courthouse, thanks to Maria Alff, Amanda Murphy and Aaron Schnitizer.

I am happy and grateful that I had the opportunity to reminisce with Hal Fillinger Jr. about his father, Dr. Hal Fillinger.

Thanks to Carol Deaver for sharing her memories of the Vogenberger farm and to retired Bucks County Detective David Hanks for taking time to discuss the Vogenberger murder case.

I thank Lynn Rosen, manager of Barnes & Noble in Philadelphia, for her inspiring Writer's Block get-togethers that have created a community for authors in the region.

I am grateful to Roger Williams for suggesting Brookline Books as the publisher of this book. I am very fortunate to have had the opportunity to work with Jennifer Green, Declan Ingram, Elke Morice-Atkinson, Hannah Pervis, Ruth Sheppard and Lauren Stead.

I also thank authors Kathryn Caraway, Doug Hood, Deborah Holt Larkin, Larry Welborn and especially Rachel Simon and Ed Steers Jr., who took time from their busy schedules to advise me and cheer me on.

I'm grateful for friends from the *Bucks County Courier Times* who shared their memories and photos: Ed Birch, the late Mary Ann Bird, Mary Ellen Bornak, Carl LaVo, Lanny Morgnanesi, Bill Newill, Ellie Reader, Mary Ann Sircely, Karl Stark, John Sweeney and Pat Wandling.

Thanks also to three *Courier Times* editors from different decades—Danielle Camilli, Shane Fitzgerald and Sandy Oppenheimer.

I thank my friends Valerie Butler, Beth Delaney, Tom Fink, Deborah Flaherty, Jim Garrett, Br. Ronald Giannone, Karen Jessee, Fran Lane, Susan Mahler, Marjorie Minton, Betty Ownsbey, Jeanne Renshaw, Luci Robson, Ed Steers Jr., Deb Tyl, Katherine Ward and Mark Washburn for their help and encouragement.

I especially thank Anne Hillerman, the author of the *New York Times* best-selling *Leaphorn, Chee and Manuelito* mysteries. She read a 240-page manuscript to help a fellow journalist she had never met.

As I researched what happened in Trevose in 1976, I was transported back in time by stunning photos and detailed stories from reporters and photographers from the *Courier Times*, *Today's Spirit*, the *Courier Post*, the *Philadelphia Bulletin*, the *Philadelphia Daily News* and the *Philadelphia Inquirer*.

At *The News Journal* in Delaware, I thank Robert Long for bringing me up to date on police scanner technology.

At the Pennsylvania Department of Corrections, thanks go to Maria Bivens, Kimberly Grant, Susan McNaughton and Ryan Tarkowski.

I am grateful to Reverend Brian Connolly, Colette McCafferty and Cheryl Viscomi at Saint Dominic Parish in Philadelphia and Officer Eric McLaurin of the Philadelphia Police Department.

I thank true crime blogger Jason Lucky Morrow for sharing his contacts.

At the Washington Crossing Council of the Boy Scouts of America, I appreciate the help of Christine Serino and Magne Gundersen.

Librarians always help researchers find their way, and I thank Lisa Frank of the Brandywine Hundred Library, Yvonne Garcia of the Los Angeles Public Library, Mary Jones of the New York Public Library, Josue Hurtado and Kimberly Tully of the Temple University Libraries and Dana Barber, Marie Dennis, and Lillian Kinney at the Margaret R. Grundy Library.

I am wildly fortunate to be represented by the Sandra Dijkstra Literary Agency. I'm especially indebted to my agent, Jill Marr, for her publishing expertise and her enthusiasm for this story. Her ideas, along with suggestions from Jake Lovell at Dijkstra, made this book immeasurably better.

I'm thankful for all the help and encouragement I received from my family members—Patrick Canavan, Bobby Green, Judy Green, Kathryn Jones, Dan McNeil, Kay Moyer, Anne Slaton and Frank and Phyllis Smith.

I'm especially grateful to my sons, Matt and Greg Sweeney, for sharing their writing advice and computer skills at a moment's notice.

I'm also grateful to John Sweeney, that reporter who was randomly assigned to wait outside the Abt home in the cold, dark early-morning hours after Geschwendt's late-night arrest. Although he stood outside in the snow for hours, when we returned to the newsroom, he bought me a hot tea from the vending machine in the newspaper cafeteria. We were married in 1979.

Index